3

$2.50

D1070981

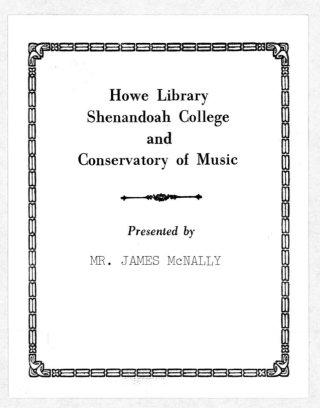

It is not by bullets and bayonets that I should recommend the attempt to be made, but by conciliation, by means suited to enlighten the Irish people respecting their rights and duties, and by conceding to them those privileges which, in common with all mankind, they have a natural and legitimate right to enjoy.

—WILLIAM COBBETT, October 1815.

Not by Bullets and Bayonets

Cobbett's Writings on the Irish Question:
1795–1835

Molly Townsend

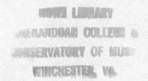
Sheed and Ward
London

Copyright © 1983 by Molly Townsend.
First published 1983 by Sheed & Ward Ltd,
2 Creechurch Lane, London EC3A 5AQ.

ISBN 0 7220 6213 3

Set by Santype International Ltd., Salisbury
Printed and bound in Great Britain
by Billing & Sons Ltd., Worcester.

Contents

Acknowledgements

Acknowledgements are due to the following for their kind permission to reprint material from copyright sources:

Ernest Benn Ltd (*A History of the English People in 1815* by E. Halevy); Faber and Faber Publishers (*Public Opinion in Ireland 1801–18* by R. B. McDowell and *The Making of Modern Ireland* by J. C. Beckett); Gill and Macmillan Ltd (*Ireland Before the Famine* by Gearoid O'Tuathaig); The Bodley Head for the print of Cobbett which appeared in *The Life and Times of William Cobbett* by Lewis Melville); the British Library for the reproduction of Daniel O'Connell's letter; and the Mansell Collection for the print of an Irish cottage.

Introduction

I want to thank you most heartily for all the good – the unmixed good you have done for Ireland, and the still greater good your visit and your knowledge of the state of the country must produce. Accept my warmest thanks in the name of and on behalf of Ireland – and believe me always, with sincere regards, very faithfully yours, DANIEL O'CONNELL.[1]

So wrote the Great Liberator of Ireland to his English Parliamentary colleague, the political writer William Cobbett, in November 1834. Outside England Cobbett is little known. Inside England he holds an honoured place in literature as the author of 'Rural Rides', a collection of essays describing his journeyings through the length and breadth of England in the 1820s. Inside and outside England his writings on Ireland have been almost totally neglected. His Letters from Ireland have all the honesty and freshness of vision of his English 'Rural Rides', but they tell a story so appalling that their neglect is understandable.

Though an intensely political book, 'Rural Rides' appeals to English readers chiefly for its non-political asides – its lyrical descriptions of the countryside, its idiosyncratic comments, and its powerful evocation of a parochial England that, even then, was beginning to pass away. But each 'Ride', like each Letter from Ireland, was originally published as one article among many in Cobbett's great weekly periodical, the *Political Register*. The *Register* was, as its name implies, a newspaper that recorded and commented on events in the political world. It included reports of parliamentary debates, exposures of mismanagement and corruption in high places, extracts from other newspapers, and correspondence from readers. It had an enormous circulation for its time and was read by dukes and factory workers, foreign visitors and cottagers. It was for Cobbett that Hazlitt coined the phrase 'a fourth estate in the country' (meaning thereby an institution

1

ranking in influence with the three great estates of King, Lords and Commons), and not, as is commonly supposed, for the press as a whole.[2]

Cobbett's rides through England were undertaken to inform himself at first hand of the state of the country so that he might be prepared to stand for Parliament. He toured Ireland after he had taken his seat in the Commons so that he could more effectively champion the cause of her suffering people on the floor of the House. It is Cobbett's tragedy that he is remembered more for his asides than for his concerns. It is part of Ireland's tragedy that in the period which culminated in the devasting famine of the late 1840s, Cobbett's warnings went unheeded and his recommendations went untried.

Cobbett toured Ireland during the Parliamentary recess of 1834. He arrived in Dublin in September and travelled extensively through the country before returning home at the end of the year. Though his letters speak for themselves in giving us a picture of the state of Ireland at the time, the sense of outrage that throbs through each one of them can be understood only if the reader is aware, as those who subscribed to the *Political Register* were aware, of the years of misgovernment which had produced the misery. For Cobbett had been reporting on the sufferings of the Irish people and crying out against successive governments' handling of Irish affairs for forty years before he saw the country for himself. The first part of the book gives an account of his long quest to discover the causes of the widespread misery and discontent that prevailed in Ireland throughout his lifetime.

The second part is based on Cobbett's description of Ireland which he published week by week in his *Political Register* during his tour of the country in 1834. Before his visit he had published in his newspaper a number of Open Letters addressed to the powerful and the great on the subject of Ireland – Prime Ministers, Secretaries of State, the King and the Pope himself. It is a mark of his genius as a

2

journalist that when confronted with the nightmare that was Ireland, he turned right about and addressed his letters to an unknown agricultural worker in the south of England. Diligent as he had been in publishing reports on the state of the Irish people, the reality exceeded his worst imaginings. The shock to his readers when they opened the Register on September 27th, 1834, and read that first letter from Dublin, headed 'To John Marshall, Labourer', and bluntly beginning:

Marshall,
I have this morning seen more than one thousand of working persons, men and women, boys and girls, all the clothes upon the bodies of all of whom were not worth so much as the smock frock that you go to work in . . .

must have been tremendous. The poignancy of it can make one weep even today.

The letters, of course, were not written for John Marshall. They were addressed to the readers of the Register who straddled all classes in society, and their purpose was to shock and shame England into a radical reappraisal of her attitude to Ireland. Cobbett's choice of his own labourer as his 'correspondent' was a journalistic device and a clever one. It highlighted the contrast between the conditions of the working classes in the two countries: by making the reader aware of the humble position of the English labourer he was addressing, Cobbett made the plight of his counterpart in Ireland more dramatic; and by stressing the concern of master for servant, he condemned by implication the absentee landlords of Irish estates.

In the seven months remaining to him between his return from Ireland and his death in June 1835, Cobbett continued to fight in Parliament and the press for all the labouring people in the United Kingdom. Although he was now nearing his seventy-second birthday, and suffering from periodic inflammations of the throat, he attended Parliamentary debates, staying up when necessary until the early hours

3

to vote, he continued to write and publish the *Political Register*, and he wrote three major works: his 'Legacy to Peel', his 'Legacy to Parsons', and his 'Legacy to Labourers'. Much of what he wrote in this last period of his life was inspired by what he had witnessed in Ireland, and the last part of the book details Cobbett's specific proposals for ameliorating the lot of the Irish poor, his condemnation of the remedies currently being proposed in Parliament as utterly inadequate to the real problem, and his passionate plea that the wrongs done to Ireland should be frankly acknowledged and justice be done to that 'at once fine and miserable country' over the water.

Many years before he visited Ireland, Cobbett had enjoined one of his sons to 'uphold the cause of truth and justice, to afford protection to defenceless innocence, and to bring down vengeance on lawless oppression'.[3] The story of Cobbett's concern to publish the truth about the innocent and defenceless victims of oppression in Ireland is one example of how faithfully he strove to put those precepts into practice.

Part 1

Cobbett Speaks out

On Rebellion and Repression
On Distress and Discontent
On Catholic Emancipation and the Protestant Church
'as by law established'

On Rebellion and Repression

. ... the rags seem the very refuse of a rag-shop, and are disposed on the bodies with such ingenious variety of wretchedness that you would think nothing but some sort of perverted taste could have assembled so many shreds together. [Sir Walter Scott.][1]

Many visitors to Ireland during Cobbett's lifetime (1763–1835) were struck by the multi-coloured rags that clothed the backs of the Irish poor. Newcomers to this period of Irish history will be equally struck by the variety of strands that run in and out of Irish politics during the revolutionary and counter-revolutionary years that it embraces.

America's War of Independence (1776–1783) and its successful outcome inspired Irish patriots to press for greater independence from Britain in the 1770s and 80s. In the 90s the call for liberty and equality crossed the Irish Sea from France and for a short time united Catholics and Protestants in a common cause. But there were also reactionary forces at work. The ever present threat of a French invasion of Ireland during the anti-Jacobin and Napoleonic wars (1793–1815) resulted in unceasing efforts by Britain to crush any signs of discontent in Ireland. When peace came after Waterloo, the widespread depression and unrest that followed it frightened the British government into harsh measures of repression at home and inevitably tended to harden its attitude to discontent in Ireland.

Cobbett was only thirteen years old when the American colonists demanded their independence from Britain. Working as a gardener's boy and then on his father's small farm in the south of England, it is unlikely that its impact on Ireland made any impression on him. Yet even in a small town of rural England, the great phrases of the Declaration of Independence: 'We hold these truths to be self-evident: that all men are created equal', did not pass unheard.

7

Writing of his boyhood, Cobbett said he remembered hearing his father espousing the cause of the American colonists and drinking a toast to the success of George Washington's armies during the War of Independence. 'My father', he wrote, 'had only to represent the King's troops as sent to cut the throats of a people, our friends and relations, merely because they would not submit to oppression, and his cause was gained'.[2] The seeds of a determination to oppose oppression were sown early in Cobbett's life.

The French Revolution affected Cobbett in a very different way. By then he had left home and was serving with the British army in Canada. At the age of twenty-eight he obtained his discharge and spent nine months in France during the moderate period of reform before the French King was overthrown. From France he went to America, and he settled in Philadelphia where he lived for eight years from 1792 to 1800.

He earned his living at first by teaching English to Frenchmen who were at that time fleeing from France, and so was in a unique position to hear from the emigrés of the excesses being committed in France during the years of the Terror. American opinion was deeply divided. Some Americans, remembering the aid given to them by France during their recent war with Britain, were clamorous for America to repay her debt to France by supporting the French Republic in her war with England. Others, frightened by the guillotinings and massacres raging in France, were adamant that the United States should remain neutral in the European war, and it was with this second party that Cobbett's sympathies lay.

The enthusiasm of the pro-French party in the United States for the French Revolution horrified Cobbett, ex Sergeant-Major of the British army.

> the delirium seized even the women and children; the former began to talk about liberty and equality in good masculine style; I have heard more than one young

woman, under the age of twenty, declare that they would willingly have dipped their hands in the blood of the Queen of France. A third part of the children, at least, were decorated, like their wise sires, in tri-coloured cockades. 'Dansons la Carmagnole', pronounced in a broken accent, was echoed through every street and alley of Philadelphia, by both boys and girls. Some ingenious democrat poet had composed the following lines:

> Englishman no bon for me
> Frenchman fight for liberty.

Poor devils! thought I when I used to hear them, little do you know about liberty![3]

Cobbett's abhorrence of the brutalities of the French Revolution led him to take up his pen to denounce the pro-French party in the United States and to urge Americans to forget their old hostility against Britain. In pamphlets and periodicals, Cobbett supported the British government in its war against the 'anarchical and blasphemous principles' of the French Republic. He adopted the pseudonym of Peter Porcupine and soon became one of the most widely read political journalists in Philadelphia, then the capital of the new republic of the United States. It was as Peter Porcupine that he first wrote about Ireland.

It was while Cobbett was making his name as a writer in Philadelphia that the democratic and republican ideals of the American and French revolutions found root in Ireland. Under the name of United Irishmen, Protestant and Catholics in Ireland joined forces calling for radical reform, full religious toleration, and a more equal distribution of wealth and power. Fearful of a full scale revolution, the British government sent an army to Ireland of over one hundred and thirty thousand soldiers from Britain to pacify the country and terrify the people into submission. The harsh measures used by the troops to quash the incipient rebellion and punish the leaders, the fact that the United Irishmen were in close contact with the French Republic, and the support which the French were giving to the Irish rebels, all com-

9

bined to excite great sympathy for the United Irishmen among the pro-French party in the United States. Members of the United Irishmen fleeing to America were hailed as heroic fighters for freedom, but Cobbett shared none of this enthusiasm. Convinced that the United Irishmen were contemplating a revolution in Ireland as bloody as that taking place in France, Cobbett defended the measures taken by Britain to crush the budding rebellion and to expel its leaders.

> Shall we blame the British then, shall we call them tyrants and slaves because they have driven from them these dis-organizing reformers who agreed in nothing but doing mischief; and who would, ere now, have spread atheism and terror through the land and filled it with its bloody tribunals, prisons and executions? Shall we applaud, shall we hug to our bosoms, these political serpents? No; let America be what heaven seems to have designed it for, an asylum for the oppressed, but never let it be called the sanctuary of the infamous.[4]

When news reached America of the great rebellion of the United Irishmen of 1798, and of the landing of French troops in Ireland to assist in the uprising, Cobbett did what he was to do so many times later in England: he published an eye-witness account of what was actually happening in Ireland. The story he published in his newspaper, *Porcupine's Gazette*, was told in the words of a member of the United Irishmen who joined the French liberation army which landed in Killala Bay in August 1798. It purported to be the confession of a Martin McLaughlin who was captured by the British while fighting with the French, and who was awaiting execution for his part in the rebellion. Cobbett published it because it seemed to justify the stand he had taken in denouncing the aims of the United Irishmen and their liaison with France.

McLaughlin told how he joined the French shortly after they had landed in Ireland. He and his friend Billy Rourke were given uniforms and muskets and drilled by a large black

West Indian sergeant, a freed slave who had joined the French army. Here is how McLaughlin described his first day.

> Poor Billy Rourke, who had taken a hearty glass on the road and was a little top-heavy, happened to drop his musket in shouldering it, and when he stooped to pick it up, the black villain gave him a terrible blow with the flat of his sword, between the shoulders, which almost tumbled him to the ground. Billy immediately snatched up his musket, and being a very strong fellow, gave the black villain a blow with the butt end of it, which levelled him to the ground and broke the musket; and while Billy stood over the sergeant, and was going to give him a finishing stroke with the barrel of the piece, a French officer stepped up and shot him through the head. I then began to think Billy was a little mistaken when he said 'that the French were our best friends'.[5]

McLaughlin and other Irish volunteers were then set to work to dig trenches, and at the end of the day sent out to forage, returning with their booty to the camp 'followed by the curses of the poor creatures all round whom we had robbed'. The final humiliation came when he and his friends were harnessed to a gun which they had to drag many miles across the hills, 'and when any one of us slackened, a stroke of the rattan or a prod of the bayonet, was sure to make him step out'. McLaughlin took part in two battles – Coloony, where the rebels were successful, and Ballinamuck where they were defeated. In this last extract McLaughlin tells the story of his capture and repentance.

> The Frenchmen who remained alive after the battle were about 850 in number; they gave themselves up as prisoners of war and their lives were spared. If they had fought like men, instead of throwing down their arms, we should not have been so shockingly cut up; at least some of us might have escaped into the hills; but instead of this, they fired at some of our boys who were running away both at Coloony and Ballinamuck. I am almost mad when I reflect on the horrors which this short but dreadful rebel-

11

lion has brought about. I became a thief and a rebel, and was harnessed like a beast and a slave; I have brought sorrow and persecution on my wife, poverty and shame on my helpless children. I shall suffer death tomorrow, as a small atonement for my guilt, and I hope God will have mercy on my poor soul, through the merits of my blessed Redeemer. Amen.[6]

A year after he had published this story, Cobbett returned to England. The year was 1800, Cobbett was now thirty-seven, and he received a warm welcome from the British government. Some of his American pamphlets describing the horrors of the French revolution had been reprinted in England as war propaganda, and his support of Britain while he was in the States merited for him in the words of one Member of Parliament a statue of gold. He was offered the editorship of a government newspaper but, having used his independence as a journalist to good effect in America, he refused and started his own journal the *Political Register* which he produced almost without interruption until his death in 1835.

Cobbett knew little about British politics. He had lived on his father's farm until the age of nineteen and since then had been almost continuously abroad in Canada, France and the United States. What he knew about England was based on a happy childhood in the country; what he believed about England was that it was standing, virtually alone, against one of the cruellest tyrannies known – the France of Marat, Danton, Robespierre and Brissot.

After his return to England, Cobbett not only continued to denounce the aims of the United Irishmen; he denounced the British government for not taking effective measures to suppress them. In 1803, Robert Emmett, again with promised aid from France, tried to rekindle the old enthusiasm in Ireland. His call for a nation-wide rebellion, however, fell on the ears of a frightened and divided nation, and the uprising was confined to a small skirmish in the streets of Dublin.

12

Cobbett castigated the government for being unprepared even though they had had warning of the plot and were aware that France had promised assistance. On the very day of the insurrection, Cobbett reported, soldiers of the British garrison in Dublin had been sent out of barracks to help with the harvest, and a messenger bringing tidings of the plot was snubbed only a few hours before the people took to the streets.

The government in Ireland was as completely surprized as a drunken sentinel, who is sleeping upon his post, and needs a good bastinado to bring him to his senses.[7]

However, by the end of the year, Cobbett's suspicions were aroused by contradictory statements from the government. At the same time as they were dismissing Emmett's rebellion as a 'contemptible riot', they suspended Habeas Corpus in Ireland and imposed martial law on the country. The speech from the throne at the opening of Parliament in the autumn of 1803 spoke of 'perfect tranquillity and quiet' reigning in Ireland, yet in December ministers were talking of 'the spirit of rebellion and insurrection to be now continually raging in Ireland'.

The bills passed by Parliament imposing martial law and suspending Habeas Corpus in Ireland shocked Cobbett. As a former soldier, he knew the severity of living under martial law, and as a stout defender of the British constitution, he believed imprisonment without trial was against all the principles he was proud to boast of as a British subject. Indeed, in his writings in America, among the reasons he gave for condemning the French republic and extolling the British monarchy was that the former violated the bastions of liberty, while the latter maintained them. In December 1803, only five months after Emmett's uprising, he made his position clear to his readers. Here he is speaking of bills before Parliament extending the duration of martial law in Ireland and continuing the suspension of Habeas Corpus.

13

These bills will not, it is hoped, pass this time without some enquiry as to the grounds on which they are to be justified, which enquiry would, of course, enable Parliament to judge of the real state of Ireland. To the bills there is no objection, if the necessity of them is made out; but every man who retains in his bosom any attachment to real liberty, or any regard to justice, must deprecate the adoption of such a measure, till it be *proved* that the case is more than a 'contemptible riot'.[8]

Having served in the British army for eight years, Cobbett was aware of the inefficiency of many of the officers, and the brutality and drunkenness common in the ranks. He had reported in his writings in America the outrages committed by the French revolutionary armies in Europe, and the summary justice meted out to their own countrymen by the American Federal forces when a rebellion against taxes broke out in Pennsylvania (the so-called Whiskey Rebellion of 1784). He knew therefore the kind of sufferings that martial law would impose on the Irish people, and he would have understood only too well the implications of the remark attributed to the Duke of Wellington when reviewing troops sent to fight in the Peninsular War in the early 1800s: 'I don't know what effect these men will have upon the enemy, but, by God, they terrify me'.

In 1805 Cobbett's attack on the government was more direct. This time the ministers added an additional reason for keeping the insurrection acts in force – the presence of Irish soldiers in the French army. Ever since penal laws were imposed in the early eighteenth century, Catholics, unable to enter any profession in their own country, had offered their skills to European powers. 'When', asked Cobbett, 'were there not Irish regiments in the French service? Yet did that circumstance ever embolden a minister to come to Parliament for a suspension of the Habeas Corpus Act?'.[9]

As Cobbett watched Parliament in his capacity of editor of a political journal, the more he saw of its workings, the stronger became his conviction that England was being governed by a corrupt oligarchy who sought only to feather their own nests at the expense of the ordinary people of the Kingdom. It was at this time that he began to attack the very basis of the government – the system of buying and selling seats in Parliament, the wholesale bribery prevalent during elections, and the corruption manifested in the distribution of pensions and sinecure posts to those willing to support the government in power, be it Whig or Tory – all of which he damned under the name of Boroughmongering and those who participated in it as Boroughmongers.

Cobbett's change of opinion from a champion of the British government to that of one of its harshest critics was due to many causes and by no means the least important was its policy in Ireland. The early period of his writings both as Peter Porcupine in America and in the early years after his return to England has often been termed his Tory period. This, I believe, to be a misinterpretation of his sentiments. Only if one holds that all those who love their country and wish to see it great are, by definition, Tories, can one apply the term to Cobbett. He certainly believed England (and as we will see later, Ireland too) to be one of the finest countries and its people among the finest of peoples in the world. But for Cobbett there was only one criterion by which a country can be judged to be great – the well-being of its ordinary citizens. He had been a proud subject of the King during his service in the army and while he was in America, but when he returned to England and saw the workings of the government which he had been extolling, this pride turned to a feeling of shame. He came home to continue his fight to defend England from the damnable principles of the French Revolution, but, as one of his biographers, G. K. Chesterton, said, it was not long before he decided 'to waste no more time on saving England from the French. He had the huge task of saving England from the English';[10] and 'England' included the whole of the United Kingdom.

I have never been able, for one single moment, to look upon Ireland or Scotland, other than as parts of my native country. I have never been able, for one single moment, to view an Irishman as other than as my own countryman. Therefore I have always considered the wrongs done to Ireland (and they are beyond all number and beyond all magnitude); I have always considered these wrongs as participated in by myself.[11]

Towards the end of his life, Cobbett made an interesting distinction between patriotism and loyalty. He defined patriotism as a love of one's country which expressed itself as a wish to see all one's countrymen prosperous and happy; whereas those who express loyalty to their country are for the most part those who, having some measure of privilege in society, support their government in order to retain their privileges.

These last paragraphs anticipate the story of Cobbett's defence of the Irish people. But to understand what follows, it is important to remember that Cobbett had roundly condemned the United Irishmen and their rebellion of 1798, and Emmett's rebellion of 1803. His writings on Ireland from about 1805 onwards can be seen in part as an attempt to make good the injustice he felt he had done to the Irish people when he was unaware of the history of the country and of the sufferings the Irish endured at the hands of the English. (Cobbett was, incidentally, radically to revise his opinions of the French Revolution when he learnt of the injustices suffered by the labouring people of France under the Ancien Régime, though he never condoned the excesses of the Revolution.) This desire to make reparation for what he had written previously, added to his feeling that the Irish were his fellow-countrymen, give to all Cobbett's writings on Ireland a passionate eloquence.

When a new Irish Insurrection Bill containing yet more sweeping powers to quell disturbances passed through Parliament in 1807, Cobbett spelt out to his readers the measures it contained. Among them were: a right to impose a curfew from sunset to sunrise; the right of a magistrate or army officer to make a forcible entry into any house at night to see if the inhabitants were at home, and to imprison any who were not; the power of any judge to dismiss complaints of misconduct by troops if he, and he alone, considered the complaint unwarranted.

Although Cobbett understood that these measures were intended to protect England from an attempted invasion through Ireland, he urged his English readers not to hate the Irish simply because they happened to live in an island adjacent to England. You are, he told his readers, 'angry with the Irish because ... because what? Angry with them because they are alive and have a desire to enjoy life?'[12] Then, referring to the harsh measures in the Insurrection Act, 'How should you like it, I say? Pray do not answer me by talking about the necessity of such laws. What I want to know of you at present is how should *you* like to lead this sort of life?'[13]

This sort of life was vividly illustrated a year later when Cobbett published the narrative of a Mr. Roger O'Connor who lived near Bantry Bay at the time when a French fleet coming to the aid of the United Irishmen was sighted off the coast. This was one of the expeditions sent by France before 1798 which failed to make a landing. Roger O'Connor, far from being a sympathiser of the United Irishmen or of the French Revolution, had housed and fed at his own expense the militia sent to repel them. Cobbett introduced his story in these words:

I shall submit the Narrative to my readers beseeching them to reflect that Irishmen are not only men as well as themselves, that they have not only feelings as well as Englishmen; but that Englishmen possess no rights to the enjoyment of which Irishmen are not fully entitled, and that to deny this proposition is to declare open war against the people of Ireland and fully to justify every act that they have, or may, commit in hostility to England.[14]

During the repression that followed this abortive attempt by France to invade Ireland, Roger O'Connor was falsely held on suspicion of aiding the rebels and imprisoned. No information against him could be produced so he was released after seven months. He was rearrested, again without evidence, for Habeas Corpus was suspended, and held in different prisons over the country for two more years. On his eventual release he found his house and land in ruins, having been destroyed by troops who had been billetted there. Cobbett ended the narrative with this appeal:

> Reader, if you be an Englishman, say how should you like to be treated as Mr. O'Connor was? How should you like to have your house, your gardens, your fields, your plantations laid waste and destroyed? How should you like to be hurried from prison to prison, to be thrown into dungeon after dungeon, and when you demanded trial, refused that trial? But surely I need not ask these questions. Well, then, is there to be no feeling for him because he is an Irishman? Are we ready to avow this to the Irish people? I trust nòt: I trust we shall prove to that unfortunate people that we feel for them as for ourselves; that we are as ready to resent their wrongs as we are our own; that, in a word, we regard them as our countrymen and that we are resolved to consider their enemies as our enemies. This is the way to produce an union; a real union; an union of the hearts of the people of the whole kingdom; and this sort of union it is that the Boroughmongers and their hirelings would wish to prevent. They have caused the people of England to believe that those of Ireland were bent upon a surrender of their country to France. What evils have not sprung from this accursed source? I beseech the reader to consider that it is not in nature that the people of Ireland should not hate us, if we persist in our credence to these calumnies.[15]

Throughout Cobbett's lifetime coercion and insurrection Acts followed one upon the heels of another, and throughout his life Cobbett raised his voice to condemn them. It was his passionate desire to see 'a real union of the hearts of the people of the whole Kingdom' that led him to protest that it

18

was not by bullets and bayonets that reconciliation could be effected, and it is from the following passage that the title of this book has been taken.

It is not by bullets and bayonets that I should recommend the attempt to be made, but by conciliation, by employing means suited to enlighten the Irish people respecting their rights and duties, and by conceding to them those privileges which, in common with all mankind, they have a natural and legitimate right to enjoy.[16]

On Distress and Discontent

We have been a little idle, in respect of Irish remedial measures, for two centuries back! In fact, ever since Oliver Cromwell's time, we have done little but grimace and make-believe, and sham a kind of governing there: imagining (miserable criminals that we have been) that falsities and injustices, well varnished, would do instead of facts and continuous performance according to the eternal laws. [THOMAS CARLYLE.][17]

Cobbett's sympathy for the Irish people stemmed not only from his sense of outrage at their being continuously subject to martial law. Ever since his suspicions had been aroused by the conflicting statements of the government on the state of Ireland, he had set to work to enquire into the reasons why the Irish people were in a continual ferment of unrest. The picture of Ireland painted in much of the English press was one of an ignorant and barbarous people riddled through with secret societies which flouted the law by means of murder, intimidation and arson.

Born of peasant stock himself, Cobbett had a natural liking and respect for the agricultural labourer, and he found it impossible to believe that such widespread discontent could occur without good reason. His doubts were fuelled by his discovery that the England he had been praising in the United States was a very different country from the one he had left some twenty years before. He saw small farms being bought up by merchants who had made fortunes by war profiteering, the enclosure of common lands robbing the cottagers of their age old rights of grazing and collecting firewood, and the heavy burden of indirect taxation borne by the poor, including the notorious window tax mentioned in the passage below. Speaking of the great change which had occurred in his absence, he said:

it has almost extinguished the race of small farmers; from one end of England to the other, the houses which formerly contained little farmers and their happy families, are now seen sinking into ruins, all the windows except one or two stopped up, leaving just enough light for some labourer, whose father was, perhaps, the small farmer, to look back upon his half-naked and half-famished children, while, from his door, he surveys all around him the land teeming with the means of luxury to his opulent and over-grown master. Is this not so? Will any man say that it is not?[18]

If this was happening in England, it was only natural for Cobbett to suppose that conditions in Ireland might indeed be even worse, and he resolved to find out the truth and publish it.

During Cobbett's lifetime, Ireland, in common with many other northern European countries, experienced a phenomenal rise in population. From about two and a half million in 1767, it rose to five million in 1800 and reached around eight million at the time of Cobbett's death in 1835. The resultant land hunger was made worse by the conversion of much arable land to grazing, so diminishing the demand for labour, and by the lack of capital in Ireland to create manufactories. Even cottage industry (weaving and spinning) gradually declined when it was exposed to competition from goods mass-produced in England and Scotland.

With little demand for his labour, the Irish peasant had no option but to accept a small plot of land which he paid for by working for its owner. From this land he had to procure enough food to support his family. As population increased, the demand for land increased, plots were divided and sub-divided, and an ever greater number of labourers became totally dependent on a small piece of land for survival. On this he grew potatoes for this was the only food that, in his ignorance and poverty, he knew would be sufficient to keep his family alive. When this failed, as from time to time in different districts it was bound to fail, the labourer with no cash income faced starvation. The recurrent famines were not due to any shortage of food because throughout the first half of the nineteenth century agricultural produce in Ireland was constantly increasing. Thousands of tons of wheat, quantities of hogsheads of butter, and more than half a million pigs were exported annually from Ireland, and the people who had helped to raise it saw it laden on wagons and taken to the docks under military escort while they themselves were in indescribable distress. The final catastrophe in the late 1840s, when, owing to potato blight, one million people died of hunger and disease, was not an unprecedented event. The difference between those years and the ones that preceded them was one of quantity, not of quality. The writer William Carleton intervenes in his novel *The Black Prophet*, based on the particularly severe famines of 1817 and 1821, to say:

> Much is said, and has been said, concerning what are termed Years of Famine, but it is not generally known that since the introduction of the potato into this country, no year has ever passed which, in some remote locality or other, has not been such to the unfortunate inhabitants.
>
> The climate of Ireland is so unsettled, its soil so various in quality, and the potato so liable to injury from excess of either drought or moisture, that we have no hesitation in stating the startling fact of this annual famine as one we can vouch for, upon our own personal knowledge, and against the truth of which we challenge contradiction.[19]

At this period of Irish history, the peasant had no one to look to for redress and no poor laws to give him relief. Most of the estates were owned by members of the so-called Protestant Ascendancy.[20] During the Reformation in the sixteenth and seventeenth centuries, the refusal of the Irish to abjure their religion or renounce their allegiance to the Pope was used as an excuse by Britain to confiscate huge tracts of land from the native Irish and parcel them out to settlers from England. Although many of these families had owned land in Ireland for a century or more by the beginning of the nineteenth century, they were alienated by language, religion and education from the main body of the people. The French historian, Elie Halévy, explains the results of such a system of

22

landowning. Neither an Englishman nor an Irishman, his words can be taken as an impartial statement of the facts.

Too few in number to organize any social life worthy of the name, the landlords did not live on their estates. They spent as much time as possible, sometimes their entire life, in Dublin or London, at watering places, or perhaps on a country estate they might happen to possess in England. Without any attachment to the soil, the landlords' one thought was to extract with a minimum of trouble the maximum of money from a population as widely separated from themselves in their ways of life as Jamaican negroes from the slave owners who exploited their labour. The landlord erected no building on his property, spent nothing to keep it in good condition; it was naked soil, or very little more, that he let to his tenant.[21]

So absentee landlords, who appeared to care nothing for the distress to which their tenants were exposed, aggravated the discontent. They were looked upon by the native Irish as usurpers of their lands, foreigners in outlook and language, and heretics in religion. Nor was this all: in addition to paying rent to a distant and negligent landlord, the Irish Catholic had also to pay tithes to support a church to which he did not belong. However small his plot of land, one tenth of all its produce was taken away to support the Protestant Church of Ireland which had few adherents in the country, and whose clergymen were often themselves absentees. An Irish historian writing in 1812 painted a moving picture of a 'half famished cotter' unable to pay his tithes:

. . . judge what his feelings must be when he sees the tenth part of his potatoe garden exposed at harvest to public *cant*; or, if he has given a promissory note for the payment of a certain sum of money to compensate for such tithe, when it becomes due, to hear the heart-rending cries of his offspring clinging round him and lamenting for the milk of which they are deprived by the cows being driven to the pound to be sold to discharge the debt. I have seen the cow, the favourite cow, driven away accompanied by the sighs, the tears, and the imprecations of a whole family,

23

who were paddling after through wet and dirt to take their last affectionate farewell of this their only friend and benefactor at the pound gate.[22]

As population grew throughout the first half of the nineteenth century, poverty and famine increased and acts of violence became ever more frequent. To quote Halévy again, 'How could the enormous army of peasants fail to revolt against the miserable lot to which they were condemned? Was it not inevitable that the barbarism to which the peasants were reduced should invest these outbreaks of fury with a character of peculiar atrocity?[23]

When Cobbett returned to England from America in 1800 he was ignorant of all the many causes of discontent in Ireland, but the years 1803 and 1804 were crucial in awakening him to some of the complexities of the Irish question. It will be remembered that after Emmett's abortive rebellion in 1803 Cobbett had condemned the administration in Ireland for being as unprepared for the rising as a drunken sentinel asleep at his post. This article inspired a correspondent in Ireland to ask Cobbett to publish in his *Political Register* a series of letters confirming and enlarging upon his criticism, and they appeared in the Register during the last months of 1803. Over the signature Juverna, the writer gave a chapter and verse account of the culpable neglect and indeed the cowardice of the civil and military powers both before and during the rising in Dublin; he also alleged that immense sums of money had been lavished 'upon ridiculous alterations and fantastic improvements at the country palaces of the Lord Lieutenant and his secretary' sums which, he asserted, would have been enough to 'pay, clothe and maintain a regiment of a thousand officers and their men for three years'; and he summed up the situation by accusing the Lord Lieutenant of heading an administration which allowed 'our people to be subject to the plunder of his clerks and our persons exposed to the pikes of the rebels'.

An attack on the administration of Ireland was ipso facto

an attack on the government in Westminster. The holders of all the major offices in Ireland – the Lord Lieutenant, the Lord High Chancellor, the Secretary of State, etc. – were appointed by the government of the day. They were lucrative posts given to friends and supporters of the government (often men with no previous knowledge or experience of Irish affairs) which changed hands with every change of government or government reshuffle. Such a damning criticism of the administration as had appeared in the Juverna letters could not pass unchallenged and in May 1804 the Attorney General brought Cobbett to court on a charge of publishing libels against the Lord Lieutenant of Ireland and others in his administration. In spite of testimony from a number of leading politicians to his good behaviour and his loyalty to the Crown, Cobbett was found guilty and fined £500. Two days later Cobbett faced a civil case for libel and was again found guilty and subjected to a further fine of the same amount.

This was not Cobbett's first appearance before a court of justice. Shortly before he left the States he had been fined by the Supreme Court of Pennsylvania for publishing libel in his American paper *Porcupine's Gazette*. On that occasion he had loudly expressed his disgust at the so-called justice meted out in the courts of law of a republican state, comparing it unfavourably with justice administered under the Crown in Britain. Now he had reason to revise his opinions. At this period criminal cases for libel were tried before a Special Jury composed of names selected by the master of the court from the common jury list. The Special Jury list had originally been created to ensure that complicated cases such as libel were tried before a jury with some educational or professional background, but it had degenerated into a body of men likely to find for the Crown. Every member of a Special Jury was paid a guinea for his attendance in court, and 'guinea men' had become a term of reproach for special jurymen who, fearing that if they found for the defendant

25

they were likely to be struck off the special list, tended to uphold the case for the Crown.

So again it was the government's handling of Irish affairs that helped to open Cobbett's eyes to that 'system' which he was to spend the rest of his life striving to reform. The very men who had welcomed him back from America as a champion of England against revolutionary France, who had offered him the editorship of a government paper, had turned against him and prosecuted him before a jury of their own choosing, because he had had the temerity to expose incompetence and corruption among their friends and colleagues. Yet Cobbett had written his article and followed it up by publishing the Juverna letters, to alert the government to the danger they faced from the French using a poorly defended Ireland as a springboard for an invasion of England. His reward was a conviction for libel: that of the negligent Lord Lieutenant of Ireland was the Order of the Garter.

The adverse judgements did not make Cobbett fight shy of publishing further letters from correspondants in Ireland. But from now on, they dealt mainly with the state of her suffering people. After his trial in 1804 Cobbett began to publish in the columns of his *Register* reports from Ireland describing the distress. One of the first was a long letter signed 'Anglo-Hibernicus' which told of 'the scanty subsistence, heart-breaking labour, mean clothing, and worse lodging'[24] to which the Irish labourer was exposed. Another described how Irish labourers were deprived of wages because all they earned was set against their rents:

> they have, therefore, scarcely any of them, anything to receive when they settle accounts, and consequently nothing to procure money to purchase fuel and clothes, except those who happen to possess a pig, which (though it would scarcely be credited in England) is fed in the same manner, and housed in the same cabbin, with their wives and children.[25]

Over the years, scarcely a month went by without some reference to Ireland appearing in the pages of Cobbett's *Political Register*. Sometimes Cobbett intervened to explain to his readers the full implications of what he was publishing. The extract below follows a report by a Catholic bishop that fourteen out of the fifteen landlords in his diocese were absentees. Here Cobbett gives a graphic description of the evils arising out of a system wherein landlords created no employment on their estates, for they never lived there; spent no money in Ireland, thus depriving the country of a demand for goods and services which a resident gentry generates; and lived in almost obscene luxury (this was the Regency period of ostentatious living), callously indifferent to the distress of those who laboured to create their wealth. Commenting on the bishop's statement on absentee landlords, Cobbett said:

> that is to say that fourteen out of fifteen of them live constantly out of Ireland, and draw away the fruits of their land, to be spent either in this part of the Kingdom or in foreign countries. The Duke of Devonshire, one of the great Whigs, has, according to his own statement, the great tithes of twenty parishes in Ireland; consequently he draws away all these great tithes. They may come in different shapes; but it is no matter whether they come in corn, in butter, in bacon, or in live cattle; still they come. A drove of hogs, or a flock of sheep, or a bale of bacon, or a barrel of butter, none of these are sent to Devonshire House; but they are sold here and the money is paid in at Devonshire House; and here they are, to be eaten by the swarms of idlers in this great place.[26]

Sometimes, and perhaps with even more effect, reports were published in the Register without comment, as was the following extract from an article in an Irish newspaper which Cobbett printed in full. It tells of the impossibility of distributing enough oatmeal to satisfy the starving people of Tulla, in Clare County.

> The Committee has been serving out this meal from six in the morning until five in the evening, and one half of the poor who attend are not supplied in that time. The pur-

chasers are so urgent in their supplications that it is with the utmost difficulty that they can be constrained by the police and yeomanry who are called in for the purpose. One woman among the crowd exclaimed: 'O Heavens! how shall I face my hungry children without a morsel to give them?' Another devoured her scanty supply raw.[27]

Until he saw Ireland with his own eyes in 1834, Cobbett had to rely on others to describe what was happening in the country. He had, however, known many Irishmen both when he was serving in the army and when he was living in the United States. This knowledge he could and did use to good effect. The government used reports of the atrocities being committed in Ireland to denigrate the Irish nation. Stories of outrages committed by secret societies which, under such names as Whiteboys, Ribbonmen, Threshers and Carders, sought to punish landlords or their agents for raising rents, to protect their members from eviction, and to protest against the collection of tithes, were reported in Parliament and the press. Cobbett questioned the assumption that the Irish were by nature a cruel people. He said that his experience of them showed them to be 'brave, generous, hospitable, laborious and full of genius. They are kind and frank in the extreme, and have been found faithful to all who have confided in them'.[28]

In April 1816 a motion was laid before Parliament for an enquiry into the causes of the misery in Ireland. The motion was negatived as unnecessary because the government declared that it was doing everything possible for the Irish people. In a speech defending the government's policies, Robert Peel, then Chief Secretary for Ireland, said that the House would see from records 'symptoms of such untameable ferocity, such systematic guilt, supported by systematic perjury, as imagination could scarcely equal'. In some parts of Ireland, he said, 'the population was in a state of depravity which baffled description'.

Cobbett reported the debate in the form of an Open Letter

28

to the people of the United States. This enabled him to point to the difference between the Irish in Ireland and the many Irishmen who had emigrated to America. 'Do you ever hear', he asked, addressing his American audience, but in reality speaking to his English readers,

> of any of this depravity, any of this untameable ferocity, any of these 'combinations against all law' on the part of these people? You want no army, no extraordinary police, no suspension of ordinary laws to keep them in order. Considering the low class of life, of which the great mass of Irish emigrants consist, my belief is, that they have surpassed in success the emigrants from any other nation. And, as to such of them as have gone to America with property or education to start with, they have certainly outstripped all others in the career of fame as well as of prosperity. Does the salt air change their nature while they are crossing the seas? What is there in Pennsylvania or New York to subdue and keep down this ferocious disposition: this disposition to combine against 'all law'? Not a single bayonet! Nothing but the constable's staff! How will Mr. Peel account for this?[29]

As an instance of the ferocity and lawlessness of the Irish, Peel had told the House the story of a magistrate who had been murdered in broad daylight to the cheers of the people who witnessed the killing. The magistrate had apprehended six men on a charge of setting fire to a house from which a tenant had been evicted, and the angry villagers had posted men along the road and shot him as he entered the village. Although a large reward had been offered for the discovery of the murderer, no one came forward, and even when one of the villagers condemned to death for another crime was offered pardon if he would give evidence, his wife begged him on her knees to keep silence because of the shame he would bring on them all if he turned King's evidence. This story, which Cobbett felt 'harrows up the very soul', was used by Peel to illustrate the depravity of a people who could thus openly condone a brutal murder. Cobbett saw it very differently.

29

Oh no! it was not in the hearts of these people, it never was and never can be, in the hearts of any district of people, to exult in what *they deem murder*. They did not deem this any more a murder than the poor woman deemed the hanging of her husband ignominious. That it was a murder is certain; that these people were under the influence of ungovernable fury is also certain; but what was it which could have produced this furious state of mind? What in all the world can have placed a people in such a state as to induce a woman who dearly loved her husband to beseech him to lose his life on the gallows rather than incur the disgrace of giving evidence against an enemy of the government? How came she to regard this as disgrace? Why, her neighbours so regarded it; and what then must be the state of mind of that neighbourhood? What must have been the causes of hatred so deep, of exasperation so terrible, as to induce a whole neighbourhood to mount upon houses, ricks and trees to behold the murder of a magistrate and to give three cheers at the firing of that fatal shot![30]

Cobbett was to find out the answers to these questions when he visited the country in 1834.

But before turning to Cobbett's own description of Ireland, it is first necessary to examine the great question of Catholic Emancipation which occupied so much time in Parliament and the press and aroused so much controversy in England during the first three decades of the nineteenth century – a controversy into which Cobbett plunged with all his customary energy.

On Catholic Emancipation and the Protestant Church 'As by Law Established'

... at the opening of the nineteenth century, Ireland possessed one of the greatest anomalies in Christendom, an established church whose adherents in a religiously minded community numbered only about one tenth of the community. [R. B. McDowell.][31]

When Cobbett began his career as a political writer, Catholics were debarred from standing for Parliament and denied access to positions of power under the Crown. The ferocious Penal Laws imposed on Irish Catholics after the victory of William III[32] over the exiled James II at the Battle of the Boyne in 1690, had been greatly ameliorated. The old laws had exiled all Catholic bishops, restricted the number of priests allowed to reside in Ireland, prevented Catholics from keeping a school or being educated abroad, deprived them of all voting rights, and had so hemmed about their ability to bequeath their property that nearly all their lands passed into Protestant hands. Most of these laws were abolished in the 1790s, and Catholics living on land worth forty shillings an acre were given the vote. They were, however, still debarred from standing for Parliament and from holding positions under the Crown.

In spite of the severity of the Penal Code, some few Catholics had managed to smuggle an education, and though the professions were barred to them, had become successful as merchants and traders. Greatly encouraged by the new climate of opinion that had led to the removal of so many of the hated Penal Laws, many of them rallied to government during the turbulent years of the 1790s, and denounced the revolutionary aims of the United Irishmen. They hoped and expected that this demonstration of loyalty to the Crown, particularly during the great rebellion of 1798, would be rewarded by the abolition of the remaining Penal Laws and to their being granted full political rights. Indeed, when the Irish Parliament was abolished after the rebellion and incorporated into the Westminster Parliament by the Act of Union of 1800, it was known that the government intended to introduce a Bill to that effect. However, opposition by the Crown and by powerful forces inside and outside Parliament, led to the proposed Bill being abandoned. The Catholics had to wait for nearly thirty years before their hopes were fulfilled.

To understand all the arguments and counter-arguments that surrounded the question of whether Catholics should be admitted to Parliament, one must take account of the prevailing attitude to the Church of Rome. Since the Reformation, many Englishmen looked upon that Church as the Scarlet Woman, the Whore of Babylon, and on the Pope as Antichrist. A Catholic was seen as an idolator, and because he continued to affirm his allegiance to the Pope and would not acknowledge the sovereign as the head of the church, his loyalty was always suspect. Cobbett described the climate of opinion when referring to his sojourn in France, then still a Catholic country, in 1792:

> I went to that country full of all the prejudices that Englishmen suck in with their mother's milk against the French and against their religion; a few weeks convinced me that I had been deceived in respect to both. I found the people among whom I lived honest, pious, and kind to excess.[33]

It is against this background of prejudice against the Catholic religion that the political struggle must be seen. After the Act of Union of 1800 which united Ireland with the rest of Britain, the debate centred on two questions: whether Catholics were sufficiently loyal to be allowed to enter Parliament; and whether it was possible, in view of the increasingly violent opposition in Ireland, to continue to force the

Catholics there to contribute to the upkeep of the Protestant Church of Ireland without returning to them some of the tithe money to provide relief for the destitute. The virulence of the No Popery faction had to be balanced against the need to conciliate Irish Catholics, because a discontented Ireland drained England of military resources and made increasing demands on the Exchequer to maintain the large garrisons stationed in Ireland to subdue unrest.

In all the arguments opposing Catholic Emancipation and insisting on the sacrosanct nature of tithes, great emphasis was laid on the need to uphold the Protestant Church 'as by law established'. Cobbett's questioning mind seized on this phrase, and he set himself the task to discover just what this law was, and why and how it came to be enacted.

Cobbett never went to school. Though he read very widely as an adult, as a child he had been, to use his own words, 'free from the frowns of a pedagogue'. An untutored mind may suffer from many disadvantages, but in one respect, perhaps, it has a superiority over the trained mind: it retains a quality of naivety which leaves it open to interpret afresh subjects which have become fossilised by over-familiarity. In enquiring into the origins of the established church, Cobbett brought this quality to the fore.

The feeling that he had been deceived about Catholicism when he went to France was as nothing to the feeling amounting almost to a revelation which accompanied his researches into the origins of the Protestant Church. For they led him to believe that the accepted version of the events of the Protestant Reformation was nothing less than a monstrous lie uttered to blind people to the true facts. Cobbett's interpretation of the events which led to the break with Rome and the establishment of the Churches of England and Ireland was that

> it was an alteration greatly for the worse; that the 'Refor-
> mation', as it is called, was engendered in beastly lust,
> brought forth in hypocrisy and perfidy, and fed and che-

33

rished by rivers of innocent English and Irish blood; and that, as to its more remote consequences, they are, some of them, now before us, in that misery, that beggary, that nakedness, that hunger, that everlasting wrangling and spite, which now stare us in the face and stun our ears at every turn, and which the 'Reformation' has given us in exchange for the ease and harmony and Christian charity, enjoyed so abundantly, and for so many ages, by our Catholic forefathers.[34]

As G. K. Chesterton said of Cobbett's writings on the Protestant Reformation, he was 'as one who had found in a dark wood the bones of his mother, and suddenly knew that she had been murdered'.[35]

In Cobbett's eyes, it was greed for the great revenues owned by the Catholic Church that was the motivating power behind the Reformation. Before the Reformation, he maintained, much of this wealth had been used by the Church to provide relief for the needy and destitute. After the Reformation, when the church lands and revenues had been confiscated and handed over to Protestants, both clergy and laity, the new owners were naturally at great pains to denigrate the Church which had formerly owned them.

> They never told us, and they never tell us, that this Catholic religion was the only religion known to our own forefathers for nine hundred years. If they had told us this, we should have said that it could not possibly have been so very bad a religion, and that it would be better to leave the Irish people still to enjoy it; and that, since there were scarcely any Protestant flocks, it would be better for us all, if the Church revenues were to go again to the original owners![36]

Furthermore, Cobbett had by now discovered that the phrase 'as by law established' had nothing to do with divine law, or even with very ancient law. It meant simply that the Church had been established by Act of Parliament during the Reformation. All the government's talk about the prescriptive rights of the clergy to their revenues, and the sacredness of Church property was sheer hypocrisy. For if Parliament had the power to take away property and tithes from one Church and give them to another, which is what it did during the Reformation, it must also have the power to do the same thing again.

All this was set out in Cobbett's book *The History of the Protestant Reformation* which was published in 1824. It traces the history of the Established Church from its inception in the reign of Henry VIII, through the times of Elizabeth, Cromwell, the Restoration and William III, and closes with the impact of the American and French Revolutions. It is unlike any history written before or since. Passionately partisan, yet meticulous in its quotations from statute books and contemporary sources, didactic in tone, yet respecting the intelligence of its readers, uncompromising in its details of atrocities, yet humorous in the midst of its denunciations, the book 'did an immense service in giving to the agitation for Catholic relief just that basis in popular support which had previously been lacking to it'.[37] Although it deals with the whole history of the Protestant Church, Cobbett refers again and again to the great injustice done to Ireland where Church property 'in which, mind, the poor had a share', had been given to Protestant bishops and parsons who had utterly failed to change the people's religion; 'and there these Bishops and Parsons are, enjoying the monstrous revenues without having scarcely any flocks'.

One last, and rather longer, extract conveys the pervading plea for tolerance and understanding of the Irish people which runs through the whole book.

> Were there, for entering on this enquiry, no motive other than that of a bare love of justice, that motive alone would, I hope, be sufficient with the far greater part of Englishmen. But besides this abstract motive, there is another of great and pressing practical importance. A full third part of our fellow-subjects are still Catholics; and when we consider that the principles of the 'Reformation' are put forward as the ground for excluding them from

their civil rights, and also as a ground for treating them in a manner the most scornful, despiteful and cruel; when we consider that it is not in human nature for men to endure such treatment, without wishing for, and without seeking, opportunities for taking vengeance; when we consider that one-third part of the people are treated as outcasts, because, and only because, they have, in spite of two hundred years of persecution unparalleled, adhered to the religion of their and of our fathers; when we consider these things, that fair and honest enquiry, on which a bare love of justice might well induce us to enter, presses itself upon us as a duty which we owe to ourselves, our children and our country.[38]

Published at the height of the controversy about Catholic Emancipation, 'The History of the Protestant Reformation' almost immediately reached a circulation of forty thousand copies; it was reprinted (and pirated) in Ireland and America, and three years after its publication in England, it had been translated into Spanish, French, German and Italian. Though little read nowadays, one sentence in it has often been taken out of context and used to condemn Cobbett as inconsistent. Cobbett ended his book with these words:

Born and bred a Protestant of the Church of England, having a wife and numerous family professing the same faith, having the remains of the most dearly beloved parents lying in a Protestant churchyard, and trusting to conjugal or filial piety to place mine by their side, I have in this undertaking no motive, I can have had no motive, but a sincere and disinterested love of truth and justice.[39]

Just as Cobbett's often repeated protestations of his love for his country have been taken to mean that he was basically a Tory, so his emphasis on his Protestant background has been taken to mean that, despite his writings on the Reformation, he remained attached to the Church of England. Both these beliefs – that at heart he was a Tory, and at heart he supported the Established Church, have made a number of his critics belittle his opinions as those of a man who held contradictory beliefs. The idea that Cobbett was a Tory has been discussed earlier;[40] the belief that he was attached to the Church of England is based on the sentence just quoted. Yet this sentence does not say that Cobbett professed the Protestant faith, only that members of his family did. In the virulent anti-Papist and anti-Jacobin climate of the time, a writer who emphasized his Protestant background would receive more attention than one who was suspected of being a Catholic or of being tainted with the deistic or atheistic principles of Thomas Paine and the French Revolution. Cobbett was so tainted. Had he not collected and published evidence to refute the rumour that Paine had retracted his writings against Holy Scripture on his death bed? And had he not, as recently as 1819, brought Paine's remains home with him from America and had the effrontery to suggest that a mausoleum should be built in England to house the bones of that wicked blasphemer?[41]

Many of the misconceptions about Cobbett, from Hazlitt to the present day, spring, in my opinion, from the difficulty of accepting that, almost alone among political writers, he began his career defending established institutions and ended it attacking them. This is so contrary to what we expect that we are inclined to look for inconsistencies in the man, when the truth lies more nearly in the fact that the man is inconsistent with our expectations. So many of the statesmen and writers of this revolutionary age (Pitt, Sheridan and Macaulay, Wordsworth and Coleridge, to name but a few) began life as reformers and ended it as staunch upholders of the established order. Even working-class radicals such as Somerville, Bamford and Place became almost 'respectable' towards the end of their lives. We expect people to modify their opinions in the light of later experience and to admit to the follies of their youth. Cobbett is no exception here: he referred to his early period as a writer as a time when he was 'a mere prater of politics'. But the period he is referring to – the heady revolutionary days which Wordsworth recalled as a time when

> Bliss was it in that dawn to be alive,
> But to be young was very heaven!

was the period when Cobbett shared in none of that enthusiasm and we find him, with his feet firmly planted on the earth, stoutly defending law and order. We do not expect a man who damned the ideals of the French and Irish revolutions to call into question, later in life, the very fabric of society – the right of landowners to their lands. We can sympathise with a man who, as he grows older, turns back to the bosom of his church; we find it disconcerting to come across a man who at the age of sixty-one turns away from it with indignation and disgust. It is the direction in which Cobbett changed that so disorients us.

Cobbett wrote his *History of the Protestant Reformation* to publicise the great wrongs done to Ireland and to inspire sympathy for its suffering people. What it actually did was to provide strong arguments for granting Emancipation to the Catholics. Cobbett was quick to see that the struggle for Catholic Emancipation was primarily a struggle of the semi-privileged to be granted full privileges, and it ignored the plight of the poor. He had, for many years, had grave doubts about the way the campaign for Emancipation was being waged. He saw it as diverting the minds of the people from the real problem – the appalling distress of the labouring classes. The most important reform for Cobbett was the replacing of the corrupt placemen and pensioners who now filled the benches of both Houses of Parliament by members who would speak for all the oppressed people of the United Kingdom.

An early move for Emancipation occurred in 1813 when Henry Gratton, an Irish (and of course Protestant) member of the House of Commons at Westminster, put forward proposals for a Catholic Relief Act. This proposal aroused strong feelings in the country which divided itself into the 'catholic' party, i.e. those who supported Emancipation, and the 'protestant' party, those who opposed it. Mass meetings were held up and down the country; Brunswick Clubs were formed to uphold the Protestant Church as by law established; even public houses hung out flags to attract people inside and offered free drinks in return for signatures to petitions. Cobbett looked on in dismay.

> One side cries out that the Church is in danger, and the other that they are persecuted for righteousness sake. One side seems to dread the faggots in Smithfield, and the other to be in bodily fear of Satan himself. That such a question does at all occupy the minds of even the most ignorant of the people, at this day, it is melancholy to think on; but that there should be men of talent so lost to all sense of shame as to come forward publickly and carry on debates on it is truly shocking.[42]

In Cobbett's view, the admission of a few Catholics to Parliament would provide no solution to Ireland's problems.

> The Catholic leaders must know, and they do know, that while Parliament remains unreformed, they will never be admitted to a share of political power; and their silence upon the subject of reform is, therefore, sufficient to make me doubt of the sincerity of their views. I say now, as I always did, that what they ask for is, of itself, nothing for the people; and if they do not ask for more, their cause ought to be indifferent to the people. It is in fact not at all a question of religion; it is a question of interests.[43]

Although expectations had been raised that some measure of relief for Catholics would be granted soon after the Act of Union of 1800, two major stumbling blocks had prevented an earlier introduction of the subject. The first was the question of the King's conscience, the second, the necessity for some safeguards to be attached to Emancipation, to make the measures more acceptable to the formidable opposition in and out of Parliament.

The question of the King's conscience arose from the fact that when James II, the Catholic king, was expelled from the throne and William of Orange invited over from Holland to succeed him, the new King was required to take an oath to

39

uphold the Protestant religion. This same oath was required of all his successors, and George III believed, or was persuaded to believe, that to allow Catholics to enter Parliament or occupy high places under the Crown, would be to violate that oath. Cobbett had no patience with this objection to Catholic Emancipation.

> It used to be the custom to keep the King's person out of sight in all disputes about political measures; but now, as often as it suits the purposes of this faction (here he is referring to the anti-Emancipation party), he is dragged forward with all the circumstances of age and infirmity, and held forth as the obstacle to such and such a measure. It is the King's *opinion*, this man now tells us, that is to settle what ought to be granted and what ought to be refused. If the King *thinks* that the thing proposed does not violate his oath, then he may agree to it; but if he *thinks* that the thing proposed does violate his oath, then he cannot agree to it. Well may the sensible part of the world laugh at us![44]

In referring to the King's infirmity and the opinion of the world, Cobbett was alluding to the well-known fact that at this time the King was suffering from recurring bouts of insanity. Within the year he was pronounced insane and his son, later to become George IV, was appointed Prince Regent.

Modern historians tend to agree with Cobbett that the use of the King's conscience as an obstacle to granting Emancipation was probably more of a political manoeuvre than a reality. J. C. Beckett writing in 1966 says of Pitt's failure to obtain Emancipation after the Act of Union:

> Though Pitt knew that the King was likely to oppose, on conscientious grounds, any political concession to the Roman Catholics, he did not regard the opposition as insuperable; and there were good grounds for supposing that the King would yield to an unanimous demand by the Cabinet . . . But the Cabinet when it came to the point was not unanimous, and the question of Emancipation was shelved.[45]

Events, too, proved Cobbett's contention correct. George IV's scruples, used later for the same purpose, were overcome in the face of a determined Cabinet when Parliament finally passed Emancipation in 1829. Another recent historian describes George IV's capitulation to his cabinet in these words: 'He had made his opposition to the measure far more public than his father had done, yet he yielded, after a monologue of an hour and a half about the story of his life, and a good cry'.[46]

The second obstacle was the question of safeguards, and it was on these that the attempt by Henry Gratton to raise the question of Emancipation failed. As was seen earlier, the fear of Popery stemmed from a more widely diffused fear of foreign influence threatening the security of the throne, and to allay such fears, it was proposed that Emancipation should be coupled with some degree of Parliamentary control of the Catholic religion. To this end two safeguards were put forward, the first that the state should be allowed to veto the appointment of Catholic bishops (who were appointed by the Pope), and the second that the state should make some provision for payment of the Catholic clergy (hitherto supported solely by contributions from their parishioners). These two provisions were termed 'The Wings'.

It is at this point that Daniel O'Connell enters the scene. Born twelve years after Cobbett, in 1775, O'Connell was the son of a small landholder and a descendant of one of the old Irish families. He was one of the first generation to benefit from the partial repeal of the Penal Laws in 1793, was admitted to the Irish bar in 1798, and quickly rose to become one of the acknowledged leaders of the Catholic cause in Ireland. When he heard of Gratton's proposed Wings, he strongly deprecated any state interference with the Catholic Church. Cobbett supported his stand. 'I think it is a Bill calculated to make the Catholic clergy the tools of the Government', he declared in 1813, and went on to state his objections to the whole charade of Emancipation. 'What boon is it to the two

41

or three millions of potato-planters and linen weavers, who have no more chance of a seat in Parliament than they have of a belly full of meat once a day?'[47]

A second bill for Emancipation proposed by another Irish member, Plunkett's Bill of 1821, was passed in the Commons but defeated in the Lords. This demonstration of growing support in Westminster roused O'Connell to enlist mass support for the cause. He founded the Catholic Association in 1823, mobilising all Catholics by asking for a subscription of only a penny a month from the poor, and toured the country to gain support.

A tall, broad-shouldered man, with an air of defiance and an eloquence at once rich and violent, O'Connell was at this time at the height of his powers. Without equal at the Irish Bar in all-round ability, his political speeches were a fascinating combination of passionate eloquence mixed with humorous anecdotes; of repetitive digressions balanced by impressive marshalling of evidence.

O'Connell's leadership was indeed crucial. He stood in a relationship to the Catholic masses that was quite unique. In this respect, at least, there was no Irish leader before or since quite like O'Connell. He shared their historic sense, their hopes and aspirations. He had no need to imagine what the experience of being a Catholic in Ireland might be. He was one of them, and he articulated in ringing phrases their deep resentment at past wrongs, and their firm resolve to make their presence felt. Balzac's comment that he (O'Connell) 'incarnated a whole people' captures in a phrase that subtle matrix of loyalties and resentments, old memories and shared pieties, which bound the Catholic peasantry to O'Connell.[48]

With strong support both financial and numerical behind him, O'Connell led a delegation to England in 1824 to protest against the repressive laws in force in Ireland and to pave the way for another attempt to press for Emancipation. While in London he naturally wished to meet the man who had so faithfully espoused the Irish cause and the meeting between O'Connell and Cobbett ended with mutual esteem.

'I spent an hour with Cobbett and was greatly pleased with him', O'Connell wrote his wife. 'He is a bold clear-headed fellow and his views are distinct and well-intentioned'.[49] Cobbett, on his side, was equally pleased and took pains to warn O'Connell not to be deceived by smooth words from the statesmen he would meet when pleading the Catholic cause. 'The very first words I said to him', Cobbett wrote, recalling this first meeting, 'were these: "Well, Mr. O'Connell, let me beseech you to bear in mind that you are come into hell, and that you have, of course, devils to deal with!"'[50]

The devils soon got to work. A third bill for Emancipation, introduced in 1825 by an English radical Member of Parliament, Sir Francis Burdett, proposed emancipation with a new proviso. The vetoeing of Irish Catholic bishops was dropped, but as well as making state provision for payment of Catholic clergy, it included a provision that forty shilling freeholders should be disfranchised and the vote restricted to £10 freeholders. O'Connell agreed to accept both these Wings, but this bill, like Plunkett's before it, was thrown out by the Lords.

O'Connell's acceptance of the two Wings on behalf of the Catholic Association aroused strong protests among many of its members in Ireland, and when the bill was defeated O'Connell publicly retracted and agreed to oppose in future both payment of the clergy and any disfranchisement clauses.

Cobbett had strongly opposed the disfranchising clause from the start. 'Irishmen', he wrote in an Open Letter to the freeholders of Ireland, "when you were paying, or giving your pennies under the name of 'Catholic rent'; and when many persons, Protestants as well as Catholics, were contributing to the same fund, did you, or did they, imagine that the money was to assist in obtaining you a *loss of your right to vote*? Did you, or did they, ever dream that 'Emancipation' could possibly mean *disfranchisement*?"[51] He roundly condemned Burdett, too, whom he had previously supported as a friend to reform. 'Can Sir Francis Burdett, that great refor-

43

mer, that friend of Universal Suffrage, really be doing this?',
he asked, and he begged the Irish to stand up for their rights
and openly denounce all the injustices imposed upon them.

The language of the Irish Catholics to the Parliament
ought to have been this: You took away the tithes and
other property of our Church; you gave them to a Protestant Clergy whom you sent hither with your Prayer
Book; you made no provision for the relief of our poor,
who were formerly relieved by our Church; you took
away from us all the means of preventing misery; your
Clergy were to convert us to the new religion; but, at the
end of three hundred years, here we are a Catholic people
still, paying tithes and Church rates to a Church which
gives us neither religion, nor relief for our poor. Let the
Catholics of Ireland make these representations to the
Parliament; let them openly and explicitly state the wishes
of their hearts. Let them do this, and they will find themselves joined by the Protestants of England; and if so
joined, they will soon look back to the days of the talk
about Catholic Emancipation, with the sort of feeling with
which the grown-up man looks back to the little fooleries
of his childhood.
    This is my advice to the Catholics. I advise them by no
means to give way to lamentation; and never again to
think of obtaining redress by humility. Their language
ought to be full of resolution, not to say indignation. Their
wrongs are without parallel in duration as well as in magnitude. Meekness never yet softened the asperity of the
wrongdoer; and my surprise is that any thing like meekness should ever be apparent in the conduct of an Irish
Catholic.[52]

When Cobbett first heard of O'Connell's admission that he
had been wrong in accepting the Wings, he called him 'that
frank, honest and unsuspecting gentleman', who really
believed that Emancipation would pass with the provisions.

To be too ready to believe, to be too ready to forgive, to
be too ready to repose confidence, are the faults of great
and generous, and not of mean and little minds.[53]

Cobbett tried to think well of O'Connell, but a further incident roused his suspicions. In a speech in Ireland O'Connell tried to exculpate himself by saying that although he himself disapproved of the Wings, he had been advised by Irish bishops to accept them. Cobbett thought this most unlikely, particularly as he had good reason to believe that O'Connell had been offered a high place in the law in return for his acceptance of the Wings. In an open letter to the Catholics of Ireland, Cobbett called on them not to believe that the bishops had deserted them:

> And you, Catholics of Ireland, trust solely to your clergy. They will never deceive you. To them the Government can promise no silk gowns, no patents of proceedings.[54]

Cobbett's faith was confirmed, for it was officially stated later that the bishops had not only disapproved of the Wings but had openly expressed their disapproval. Even then, Cobbett explained O'Connell's inconsistencies as arising more from vanity than from greed. In an article 'A Timely Warning to the Catholics of Ireland', Cobbett set out the details of his association with O'Connell and told how he had constantly urged him to approach the Government 'full of expressions of the bitterest resentment'. Yet O'Connell had given way to the blandishments of those in power and obtained nothing for his pains. 'I ascribe his mischievous assent and his more than marvellous credulity to the suggestions of his unparalleled vanity'.[55]

However, over the next three years, the failure of the Catholic Association to state openly all the grievances under which the Irish people were suffering; their failure to ally themselves with the growing movement for Reform in Britain; their conciliatory addresses pleading only for Emancipation; all these stirred Cobbett to denounce even more strongly any Emancipation movement which ignored the real sources of misery in Ireland. He began to taunt O'Connell, ascribing his espousal of the Emancipation cause to mere personal ambition. He wrote and published in his Register a satirical play entitled *Big O and Sir Glory*[56] (his new names for O'Connell and Sir Francis Burdett) in which he poked fun at all the shufflings and prevarications of the pro-Emancipation parties. O'Connell replied in kind. In a speech to the Catholic Association referring to the 'savage Cobbett', he said: 'Let not the name of this beast (for man I will not call him) be ever again mentioned in this Association if it be possible to avoid it. He is, as he should be, an outcast from all that is respectable and dignified in society, and a disgrace to the literature of the age'.[57]

During the period of the quarrel between the two men, the Catholic Association had adopted a new tactic to further their cause. This was to persuade all the forty shilling freeholders to cast their votes only for a candidate pledged to support Catholic Emancipation. In the General Election of 1826 the voters defied their landlords (there was no secret ballot then) and elected pro-Emancipation candidates in Waterford, Louth, Monaghan and Westmeath. Such a success revitalised the Catholic Association and funds were raised to compensate any voter who had been evicted from his freehold or had in any other way become the victim of 'Orange tyranny' because of the way he had cast his vote. Two years later the forty shilling freeholders made their last and triumphant defiant stand: in a by-election in Clare they elected Daniel O'Connell himself.

The British Parliament was now confronted with the problem of a Member, properly elected by its own franchise laws, who was unable to take his seat because of the exclusion of Catholics from the House.

Cobbett was naturally delighted at the discomfiture of the government. His attacks on O'Connell had throughout been written to goad him into more determined action on behalf of the people and to alert the true friends of Ireland to the uselessness of Emancipation without accompanying measures of reform. He was, though, always doubtful of O'Connell's strength to resist the blandishments which would be held out to him, and he now vehemently urged him to

46

come over at once to England and try to take his seat in the Commons, even at the risk of being imprisoned for his pains. 'He is bound to take it', Cobbett told his readers, 'and in a manner the most public and the best calculated to make his ejection conducive to the good of the people'.[58] O'Connell, however, held back, considering it more prudent to wait until the next session of Parliament, rightly believing that with his election and the prospect of many more Catholics winning seats in future, the government would be forced to grant Emancipation. Cobbett thought nothing of such prevarication.

> Do we not all know that a réchauffé, as the French call a warmed-up dish, though assisted by all the spices in the world, has never the fine relish of the first day's cookery?[59]

O'Connell stood his ground and it was not until the government brought in its own bill for Emancipation that he came to England. The Government's Bill included the same provision as Burdett's Bill: the disfranchisement of the forty shilling voters, and Cobbett was disgusted at O'Connell's silence.

> he stands quietly, even under the gallery of the House of Commons, and hears the proposition for disfranchising the forty shilling freeholders; and does not step down from the bench to demand his seat that he may defend them.[60]

The failure of O'Connell to demand his seat in Parliament immediately after the Clare election, the suspicion that he had been offered a lawyer's silk gown for accepting the Wings, his public rejection of the Wings in 1825 after the bill was defeated and his silence about them now in 1829, and the fact that he was betraying the very men who had so courageously elected him, made Cobbett launch his bitterest attack. In an Open Letter to the Duke of Wellington (himself an absentee Irish landlord), under whose premiership the Emancipation Bill was introduced to Parliament, Cobbett condemned the Wings and castigated 'O'Connell and his crew' for accepting them:

47

they have been guilty of treachery the most foul; they have broken engagements the most solemn; and they have brazened it out with characteristic impudence. The annals of the world do not exhibit two months so fertile in apostacy, perfidy, disregard of character, stupidity at the same time, and fool-like vanity equal to the last two months: and of all the heroes that have appeared on this interesting stage, your countryman, O'Connell, certainly takes away the palm.[61]

The Bill passed through Parliament; George IV wept and sulked but signed; the forty shilling freeholders were disfranchised; and O'Connell took his seat in the Commons.

Once O'Connell was seated in Parliament, the immediate cause of the quarrel between him and Cobbett was removed. Cobbett had always said that Emancipation was useless by itself; but he did believe with O'Connell that the proper place for remedying the Irish problem was Parliament and that Catholic members from Ireland were needed to plead their case. He now began praising O'Connell's speeches, hoping that by giving him support, O'Connell would address himself to the real problems of Ireland. Never one to shy away from giving advice, Cobbett boldly called on the Irish priests to help in the fight.

I know that if I were a father confessor of any man who should be a Member of Parliament and who should sit there for only twenty-four hours without making some motion for getting back to the poor their due share of the tithes, and the other revenues of the Church, never should he have absolution from me, until he had made compensation by the performance of his sacred duty; and even then I would make him count the grains of a sack of clove seed by the way of penance for his neglect.[62]

The fight was indeed more necessary than ever, for Cobbett's prophecy that Emancipation would do nothing to alleviate discontent was amply fulfilled. As early as August 1829, Cobbett reported that the result of the Emancipation Act was 'more angry feelings, more rival processions, more bloody fights, false swearings and murders'.[63] A nineteenth century Irish historian confirms Cobbett's opinion of the folly of granting Emancipation without accompanying it with a radical redistribution of the country's wealth.

The discontent and disappointment of the people (who found that emancipation did not save them from starvation) found vent in occasional deeds of violence; and always for the same old reasons – ruthless seizure for tithes, and wholesale ejectment of tenants. Many thousands of farmers now found themselves emancipated, but disenfranchised, and in imminent danger of being ejected and thrown on the highways. The grievance of tithe, and the whole of that monstrous iniquity called the Established Church, seemed to be felt by the people with even more intensity of irritation, since they were now told that they were now 'emancipated', and that there was an end of Protestant Ascendancy. What this emancipation might be, they did not well understand, and knew no other result from it than that they were deprived of the franchise and could, therefore, get no more leases. And they thought they saw Protestant Ascendancy all around them as rampant as ever. Protestant Ascendancy was always at their doors; it entered their cabins and carried off their pans and pots, their calves and pigs, to satisfy a Protestant rector. Protestant magistrates (who were in the great majority) were always ready to browbeat them from the bench, and to send policemen to search their beds for arms; Protestant jurors always met them in the courts of justice, and proved to them that the laws of the land were not for them.[64]

After Emancipation the resistance to tithes began to amount almost to civil war, and this tithe war reached its climax in the 1830s. So strong and united were the Irish in their opposition that in 1832 the new Whig government under Lord Grey applied to Parliament for extra laws to crush confederacies opposed to tithing and to enforce collection. Cobbett commented wryly:

It is not enough to make forcible entry on men's premises and seize their goods; it is not enough that the shepherd of

49

the fold of Christ take away the fleece by force and apply it, not to the clothing of the naked, but to his own profit and his own luxurious enjoyments; this is not enough, it appears, for my Lord Grey, who expresses his determination to propose that new laws should be passed of a more vigorous and effective description.[65]

As to Grey's talk of a conspiracy against tithes in Ireland, Cobbett considered this a grossly misleading use of the word, inciting fear and hatred against the Irish, when what was needed were sympathy and understanding. The Irish were refusing to pay tithes because they were starving, and their resistance was the resistance that all men show when life is at stake.

It is a conspiracy such as men enter into when they rush out of a playhouse that is said to be on fire. In short, there is no conspiracy whatever, any more than there can be said to be a conspiracy against crime of any sort.[66]

Cobbett believed that the tithes belonged to the poor as of right. The enormity of confiscating Church lands and then, under the misnomer of tithing, forcing the Catholic people to pay tribute to their robbers in perpetuity, was to him a crime. The Church of Ireland had been established by Act of Parliament. It must now be disestablished by another Act. For Cobbett, only the complete disestablishment of the Church of Ireland and the restoration of all its income to its original purpose of providing for the needy and the destitute could end Irish discontent.

During the period of the furore over Catholic Emancipation, Cobbett was attempting to obtain a seat in Parliament for himself. He stood as a Radical, calling for a reform of Parliament, universal suffrage, and an end to corruption, and his failure in Coventry in 1820 and in Preston in 1826 was in part due to his refusal to use bribery during his campaigns. At the end of 1831 he canvassed on fourteen propositions for reform and in his address to electors he set out the measures he proposed to put before Parliament and declared:

50

I am resolved not to be a member of Parliament unless those who send me thither pledge themselves to support me to the utmost in my endeavour to cause these measures to be adopted. If you do this, gentlemen, great indeed will be the glory which you will confer upon me; and, on the other hand, if neither you, or any body of electors do this, much greater satisfaction shall I derive from remaining engaged in the humble pursuits which have hitherto been the delight of my life.[67]

Among the propositions was a 'Proposition for abolishing the Protestant Hierarchy in Ireland' and in this Cobbett proposed the disestablishment of the Church of Ireland, the restoration of all Church revenues to the people, and the introduction of Poor Laws to Ireland. He was elected on his fourteen propositions by the people of Oldham in Yorkshire, and took his seat in the Commons in January 1833.

The session opened with a debate on the reply to the Speech from the Throne in which the King had asked for special powers for 'controlling and punishing the disturbances of the public peace' in Ireland. Cobbett proposed an amendment to the reply to include this statement:

We most solemnly assure your Majesty that we will never give our sanction to their being treated with injustice and cruelty and that we will, with the smallest possible delay, proceed to the consideration of means of redeeming those manifold grievances under which they have so long been suffering, and which are, we are firmly convinced, the real cause of their present unhappy disturbances.[68]

The amendment was defeated by 323 votes to 23.

In the same debate Cobbett intervened with a long speech demanding the abolition of tithes in Ireland.

I do not call taking that which I have a right to take spoilation, and the question is – has Parliament a right to deal with church property as it pleases, or has it not? It did once, I know, deal with the whole of it; it took it from one set of men to give it to another set . . . Not above forty families hold all the church property of Ireland; and I ask whether it is the interest of the gentlemen of England

51

to have their estates mulcted to the extent of two million sterling, according to the calculations of the Minister for Middlesex, to maintain an army of soldiers to compel the payment of tithes to forty families? Does religion demand it? Does the religion of Jesus Christ demand it? No – it does not.[69]

He ended with these words.

I am for totally and entirely abrogating, annulling, rendering frustrate and of no effect, the Protestant hierarchy in Ireland. Nobody can misunderstand me, I trust. I do not say so because I shall gain anything by its abolition or by its continuance. I am no parson to receive tithes – and no Quaker to refuse for conscience sake to pay them; but I know that the putting down of that hierarchy is necessary to the happiness, peace, safety and renown of this Kingdom. It can be endured no longer with security to the Kingdom or to the King's throne; therefore as a loyal subject of the King, and a faithful representative of the people, I declare my opinion against it. Look at the history of the Church, and in it you read all the great calamities of the country: to maintain it, one King was brought to the block, and another driven from the throne. What it is destined next to effect, I leave you, gentlemen, to determine; but I cannot sit down without expressing my gratitude to the House for the great attention I have received.[70]

Throughout 1833 and 1834 Cobbett and the Irish Catholic members led by O'Connell fought in vain for the Irish people. United in a common cause, the old animosity between O'Connell and Cobbett turned to mutual admiration. Cobbett described to his readers one of O'Connell's speeches against one of the many coercion bills before Parliament.

Upon this occasion, it is impossible for me to refrain from expressing my admiration of the things done by Mr. O'Connell. I never before had an opportunity of witnessing his surprising quickness, and the irresistable force of that which drops from his lips. His sincerity, his good humour, his zeal, his earnestness, his willingness to sacri-

52

fice everything for the cause of the people; for the cause of those who can never serve him in any way whatsoever; it is only necessary to be a witness to explain why it is that the people of Ireland love him and confide in him; and why it is he is so hated and detested by every one who has a tyrant's heart in his body.[71]

The Irish members, on their side, supported Cobbett. Only a very few radical members had been elected to Parliament after the Reform Bill of 1832, and Cobbett had other affairs than Ireland to put before the House. He had to plead the cause of the working people in England; to protest against the appalling conditions of the factory workers, women and little children as well as men, in his own constituency in Oldham; to expose corruption; to denounce the banking system; to present petitions.

Being sent to Parliament by the good people of Oldham, I must say I would have been of no use if I were not supported by the Irish members of Parliament. But for them, I should have been all alone; and though it would be somewhat difficult to do it, I should, I suppose, have been hooted out of the place, if it were not for the honest support of the Irish members.[72]

Although the alliance between the O'Connellite party and Cobbett continued until Cobbett's death in June 1835, there were differences of opinion as to the most effective way of relieving the Irish people from their misery. These centred on two issues: whether energies should be harnessed to working for a repeal of the Union, and whether Poor Laws should be introduced to Ireland.

The question of Repeal had been mooted ever since the Act of Union of 1800. The abolition of the Irish Parliament and the absorption of its members into the Westminster Parliament had caused resentment among many Irishmen, Protestants as well as Catholics. Cobbett, however, could not foresee any benefits arising from the restoration to Ireland of its own Parliament; such a Parliament, he believed, would be as deaf to the appeals of the Irish poor as the Parliament of the United Kingdom, even since the Reform Act of 1832, was to the appeals of the poor of the whole of the United Kingdom. He looked upon the movement for Repeal much as he had looked upon Emancipation – as a thing unobjectionable in itself, but unlikely to instigate the urgently needed reform of the whole apparatus of the Irish establishment. Furthermore, as we have seen, Cobbett believed the abolition of the Church of Ireland to be the first priority, and the advocates of Repeal were equivocal in their attitude to the established church. The O'Connellite party feared they would alienate those Protestants who were sympathetic to their cause if they demanded the disestablishment of the Church of Ireland: such a demand inevitably called into question the 'prescriptive rights' of the Church of England to its own revenues, and would unleash a flood of opposition from powerful vested interests on both sides of the Irish Sea.

So the Irish party under O'Connell concentrated their efforts on the demand for Repeal of the Union, and were actively opposed to the second question, the necessity for Poor Laws for Ireland. This question brought to light sharper differences between Cobbett and O'Connell. Cobbett believed that the needy and the destitute had an inalienable right to relief from the state. In England the Poor Laws were established during the reign of Elizabeth. After the dissolution of the monasteries and convents, the poor had nowhere to look for relief, and the Poor Laws were adopted in England when it became apparent that, as Cobbett put it, 'rebellion would never cease till a regular, a legal, and a certain provision for the indigent had been made'.

If I be asked why the poor-laws were not extended to Ireland, my answer is, that they were not established in England until the 43rd year of the reign of Elizabeth; and that they arose out of the fear of those who had become possessed of the church-property, that the people would, in the end, take that property from them, unless a never-failing source of relief were established. Then, if it be asked, how the people of Ireland came not to make the same demand, the answer is, that in all probability they did make the demand, but that the Government of England had the means of stifling their discontents, and of compelling them to live without poor-laws. This is the true history of the matter: the want of poor-laws has been the great source of all the troubles and miseries of Ireland; and therefore it is reasonable to conclude, that, do what we will besides, Ireland will never become other than a burden to England, until this Act of justice be done to its now miserable people.[73]

In 1832 Parliament began to debate a reform of the Poor Laws in England. Until this time they were mainly based on supplementing wages out of rates if they fell below an amount considered necessary to sustain an adequate living, and they were adjusted to take account of the cost of living and of the number of dependents in the family. With the vast increase in population and in unemployment, the burden of rates was becoming intolerable, and the proposed new Poor Laws 'carried out logically the ideas of those who held that pauperism was a crime, and that the right method of dealing with it was deterrence ruthlessly applied'.[74] In and out of Parliament, Cobbett strenuously opposed these measures, which included the substitution of indoor relief for the able-bodied instead of supplementing inadequate wages; and the establishment of large district Union workhouses to replace the parochial ones. These new workhouses would remove the poor from their villages, separate husbands from wives, and parents from their children, and impose hard labour and the minimum of nourishment (what Cobbett called the Coarser Food clause), in the hope of deterring people from applying for relief. It is a tragic irony that when Poor Laws were eventually introduced to Ireland in 1838, three years after Cobbett's death, they incorporated many of the harsh provisions which he had striven to prevent and against which, as we will see, he speaks out in his Letters from Ireland.

Cobbett, then, in advocating Poor Laws for Ireland, was advocating the old, relatively humane though often grossly inefficient English system. Even so, he found himself in opposition to Daniel O'Connell. Ever since the repression of the Catholic church in Ireland and the expropriation of all its property in the sixteenth century, any relief that had been provided for the destitute had been donated by charity. When famine, and the pestilence which almost invariably accompanied it, struck in a district, soup-kitchens and other methods of relief were provided from donations, often from Protestants as well as Catholics, and, when distress was widespread, sometimes from donations from English societies too. The British government, also, gave grants to schemes for public works such as road and canal building, to provide wages so that the Irish could purchase the food which was always available to those who had money to buy it. But these measures were inevitably only temporary palliatives, and were never sufficient to do more than relieve a small minority of the thousands in distress.

Yet the Irish were proud of their independence and of their generosity in times of want, and O'Connell, brought up in this tradition, believed Poor Laws depraved those who received relief. One must not forget, either, that to a Catholic, relief from the state meant relief from a hated and alien government. O'Connell maintained that the English system of providing relief for indigent old-age took away the stimulus of saving during one's working life so as to provide for the future, and militated against sons and daughters caring for their parents. He deplored the parish laws which confined people to live in their birth-place rather than risk removing from their parish and forfeiting their right to relief. In a speech in Dublin in January 1832 he said:

I have thought upon this subject by day – I have mused upon it by night – it has been the last thought that visited my pillow before I closed my eyes to sleep – and it has been the benefit of my morning meditations; and the result to which I have come is this, that it would be impossible to introduce poor laws here without enslaving and degrading the poor.

56

I prefer the wild merriment of the Irishman to the half-sulky, half-miserable tones of the English under the poor-laws. The Irishman certainly has his distresses, but then he has his hopes; he endures much misery; but then he entertains expectations of redress.[75]

Cobbett found it very difficult to accept these arguments, particularly as he felt that the Irish people had been deprived of their birth-right to relief by the confiscation of their church-lands. Moreover, he thought that a man who worked for low wages should not be compelled to go without any comforts in order to provide for his old age, and if he did manage to save 'where is the tongue or pen to speak the praise that is his due?'; he denied that the settlement laws were unpopular, holding that most people wished to stay amongst those they knew; and he pointed out that in England, sons and daughters were compelled to support their parents if they were able to do so. Only if they could not, were old people supported by the parish.

The differences of opinion between Cobbett and O'Connell never led to a quarrel, both men believing that the other sincerely had the welfare of the Irish people at heart. But it was these differences that induced Cobbett to go to Ireland to see for himself. How was he to reconcile the reports he had received from Ireland and published in his Register with O'Connell's talk of Irishmen indulging in wild merriment and of their having hopes of redress? From whence could this relief come unless absentee landlords were forced to reside and pay poor-rates, and the Church of Ireland forced to give up its monstrous revenues? In July 1834 Cobbett told his readers:

I have resolved to see this country with my own eyes, to judge for myself, and to give a true account of it, as far as I am able, to the people of England. I am resolved to go, as if to a country about which I have never said a word. I have now, for two sessions of Parliament, listened to such contradictory statements, both coming from gentlemen of unimpeachable veracity, that it is impossible I should not desire to have the evidence of the facts before me. It is impossible for me to disbelieve, wholly and entirely disbelieve, all the statements made on either side. In short, I have a desire to know the whole truth; and if I cannot get it by seeing the country, very few men can.[76]

Two months later, Cobbett set sail for Ireland.

William Cobbett writing his Political Register.

Normandy Farm, Ash, Surrey: William Cobbett's home, where John Marshall was employed.

'Rough rafters covered with old rotten black thatch' (see
page 72). An Irish cottage, from an engraving in the Mansell
Collection.

Merrion Square
20th Nov - 1834

30

My dear Sir

You may imagine how I am surrounded but I am most desirous to see you — If however must (for reasons) be here — I want to thank you most heartily for all the good — the unmixed good you have done for Ireland and the still greater good your visit and your knowledge of the state of this country must produce — I will be at home all the evening and all the morning tomorrow — and all the time — Anglice — any time you chuse

Accept my warmest thanks in the name and on behalf of Ireland — and believe me always — with sincere regard

very faithfully yours
Daniel O'Connell

Wm Cobbett Esqr
M. P.

Daniel O'Connell's 20 November 1834 letter to William Cobbett. (British Museum)

Part 2

Cobbett's Letters from Ireland

He has yet much of the hale and stout appearance for which he has been so remarkable through life. His step is wonderfully firm, and his voice is clear, loud, and articulate to an extraordinary degree. As he stood upon the balcony, with his white and silvery hairs uncovered, and read his answer to the address which was presented to him, marking each sentence with corresponding gesture and emphasis, his appearance was particularly striking, and produced a marked effect on his auditors. He wore a light grey coat which fitted loosely to his person, and duck trowsers. [From a newspaper report of Cobbett's arrival in the city, September 1834.]

Cobbett landed at Kingstown and was received and entertained by General Sir George Cockburn at his 'magnificent seat' of Shanganach near Bray. He made his public entry into Dublin on a wet Thursday morning, the 22nd of September, 1834. He was driven to the city in an open carriage through cheering crowds and, according to *The Morning Register*, 'numbers of elegantly dressed females filled the balconies of the different streets through which the procession passed, and waved their handkerchiefs as tokens of approbation. More than one honest fellow was observed to grasp with eagerness the hand of the hon. member as he alighted from the carriage, in order to have it to say that he had shaken hands with William Cobbett'. Fulsome speeches of welcome were then addressed to him and Cobbett replied in kind, ending his address in these words:

Support your members; never be afraid of tiring them with petitions, or of wearying them; they have nothing else to do. They ought to have nothing else to do, but to listen to your complaints, and attend to your wrongs. Pursue this course, and I shall live to see Ireland, as I always wished her to be, happy and prosperous.

His speech was received with long continued cheers.

Cobbett, however, had no intention of confining his visit to Ireland to a series of public addresses and receptions in his honour. He refused an invitation to stay with O'Connell at Derrinane Abbey on the grounds that it would retard his plans to tour the country which, he said, he was performing not for pleasure, but 'to discharge that duty which my excellent constituents have a right to expect from my hands'.

In his monograph on Cobbett, G. K. Chesterton said that Cobbett was above all things a man with eyes in his head who saw, not what he expected to see, but what he saw. Nowhere is this aspect of his character more evident that in these first two letters from Dublin to which he gave pride of place in the *Political Registers* of September 27th and October 4th. In these letters he takes us, as it were, by the hand through the city, seeing what he saw, asking the questions that he asked, and sharing with him his burning indignation. Yet he does not leave it there; we are not left entirely with a feeling of helplessness. In all the letters from Ireland, Cobbett tells his readers, even those in the position of his labourer, Marshall, a wage-earner deprived of the vote because he was not a freeholder, that there were some things that they could and must do. Cobbett makes his readers face facts honestly and squarely, but he never allows them to sink into impotent despair. Therein lies the secret of his power.

LETTER 1[1]

TO JOHN MARSHALL
Labourer,
Normandy Tithing, Parish of Ash,
County of Surrey

Dublin.
22 *Sept.* 1834

MARSHALL,

I have this morning seen more than one thousand of working persons, men and women, boys and girls, all the clothes upon the bodies of all of whom were not worth so much as the smock-frock that you go to work in; and you have a wife and eight children, seven of whom are too young to go to work. I have seen the *food* and the *cooking* of the food, in a LARGE HOUSE, where food is prepared for a part of these wretched people. Cast-iron coppers, three or four times as big as our largest brewing copper, are employed to boil *oatmeal* (that is, *ground oats*) *in water,* or *butter-milk,* or *skim-milk;* and this is the food given to these poor creatures. The *white cabbages,* the *barley-meal,* the *pot-fat,* the *whey,* and the *butter-milk,* which George boils daily for our little pigs and their mothers, is a dish, to obtain a mouthful of which, thousands of these people would go on their knees. Marshall, you know how I scolded Tom Denman and little Barratt and your own son Dick, on the Saturday before I came away, for not sweeping the *sleeping-place* of the *yard-hogs* out clean, and what a strict charge I

62

gave George to fling out the old bed, and to give them a bed of fresh straw every Saturday. Oh, how happy would thousands upon thousands in this city be, if they could be lodged in a place like that roughest hog bed! I this morning saw a *widow* woman and her four children, in the spot where they had slept; on *their bed*, in short. George remembers my looking over at the sows and their sucking pigs, and at the two youngest calves, just before I came away; and that I told him to keep them in that nice condition all the time that I should be away. Now, Marshall, this poor widow and her little children were lying upon a quantity of straw not a twentieth part so great as that allotted to one of the sows and her pigs; and if I, on my return, were to see, as I am sure I shall not, the straw of the calves as dirty, and so broken, as that upon which this widow and her children were lying, I should drive George out of the house, as a slovenly and cruel fellow. And this, you will observe, is the case of thousands upon thousands of persons; it is the case of whole streets as long as the main streets of Guildford and Farnham. Your pig-sty and Turvill's pig-sty, and the sties of other labouring men, are made by yourselves, with posts and poles and rods and heath, and your supply of straw is very scanty, and compels you to resort to *fern* and *dead grass* from the common: but, now mind what I say, I saw Turvill's pig-sty the day before I came off, and I solemnly declare, in the face of England and of Ireland, that Turvill's two hogs were better lodged, and far better fed; and far more clean in their skins, than are thousands upon thousands of the human beings in this city; which, as to streets, squares, and buildings, is as fine a city as almost any in the world! The LARGE HOUSE, of which I have spoken to you above, is called the MENDICITY. The word *mendicant* means *beggar*, and the word MENDICITY means *beggary*. So that this, which was formerly a nobleman's mansion, is now the *house of beggars*. From this house there are sent forth, every day, *begging carts*, drawn by women, who go from house to house to collect what is called "*broken victuals*." These carts are precisely, in shape and in size, like my *dog-hutches*, except that

63

the begging carts have a sort of *hopper* at top to put the
victuals in at, and a locked-up door at one end, to take the
victuals out of. Now mind what I am going to say: the
bones, bits of rusty bacon, rind of bacon, scrapings of dishes
and plates, left cabbage, left turnips, peas, beans, beets,
and the like odds and ends, that Mrs Kenning throws into
our *hog-tub*, form a mass of victuals *superior in quality* to these
mendicity-collections; and in proof of which I state the following facts: that the carts, when they come in, have their
contents taken out and examined by persons appointed for
the purpose, who separate all that can become food from
the mere rubbish and filth, that is, by servants at the
houses, tossed into the carts amongst it; and a gentleman
has, in evidence given by him before commissioners here,
stated, that out of *seventy odd hundred weight* taken out of the
carts the examiners found *only nine hundred weight* that could
by any *possibility* become human food, the *bones* in these
nine hundred weight not being included.

The real statement is this:

In twenty-two weeks the begging carts col- lected	273 cwt.
Of this, unfit for any use..................	175
	98
When the bones and other uneatable things were separated from this there remained, applicable as human food	9 cwt.

So that these poor women, in these twenty-two weeks,
actually dragged to this place 273 hundred weight of stuff
very little better than that which forms an ordinary town
dunghill!

Now, Marshall, I address this letter to *you*, because you
are the most able and most skilful of my labourers, though
all of you are able and good. You cannot *read* it, I know;
but, Mr. Dean will read it to you; and he will, some
evening, get you all together, and read it, twice over, to
you all. I will cause it to be printed upon a slip of paper,
and cause copies of it to be sent into all the parishes round
about our own.

You will, perhaps, think, that the *land* here is not like that at Normandy. Indeed it is not; for one acre here is worth four of that; the grass here is the finest that I ever saw in my life; six acres of it worth more than my twenty acres; and, when I go home, I shall be happy indeed to find my Mangel Wurzel and Swedish Turnips (about which we have taken so much pains) any thing like so good as those which I saw growing here, raised, too, *from seed bought of me.* Here are as fine beef and mutton as any in the world, and wheat and barley and oats in abundance. The causes of this strange state of things, I have come hither to endeavour to ascertain, and to offer to this suffering people my opinions as to the remedies that ought to be applied.

But, Marshall, I hope that none of you will believe that I lay the state of the Irish working people before you with a view of making the unfortunate amongst you *patient* under a refusal to give *you relief* according to the *ancient law*, which our fathers left us as our best inheritance. Just the contrary is the view, with which I have written this letter. There are certain savage villains, who are urging the Government and the Parliament to adopt measures to compel you to live on "COARSER FOOD" than that which you now live on; and, in short, to reduce you to the state that I have above described the Irish working people to be in; and I write this, that you may all see what that state is, and that you may be on the watch for any thing that these villains may recommend to be done against you, and that you may be ready to plead and to stand by *the law* against the recommendations of those barbarous monsters, who are seeking to live in idleness and to fatten on your toil.

Besides, it is the duty of you all to wish and to endeavour to better the lot of those Irish sufferers; and, as I shall hereafter show you, you can do much, if you will. People of property are just as kind and charitable here as they are in England: they subscribe large sums of money to prevent this misery: but there wants THE LAW, the *Christian* law, the *holy* law of England, which says that no human being shall, on English ground, *perish from want.* How there came not to be POOR-LAWS here, as well as in England, I have not now

65

time to explain to you. But here there are none; and you see the consequences. Manchester has about the same number of people as Dublin: in the former the *poor-rates*, it is calculated, hardly surpass the *subscriptions* in Dublin: yet, misery, such as is here, is wholly unknown in Manchester. It is the *law* that does all; that law, which has so long been the greatest glory of England; that law which the base Scotch negro-drivers (not the *Scotch people*, who hate them as cordially as I do) are now recommending to be destroyed; but which law, it is our duty to maintain, and, not only to maintain for ourselves, but to cause to be extended to these our fellow-subjects of Ireland.

I hope that you and your family are quite well, and that the Scotch villains will never be able to take from you the bacon and bread that you bring for your breakfast, and to put cold potatoes in your satchel in their stead.

I remain,

Your master and friend,

WM. COBBETT.

LETTER 2

Dublin,
27 *Sept.* 1834

MARSHALL,

After I wrote to you, the other day, about the Mendicity, I went again at the *dinner time*. You know, I saw the *breakfast!* that is the *ground-oats* and *butter-milk*, or *water*, or *skim-milk* (sometimes one and sometimes the other), boiling in great coppers for the *breakfast;* and now I went to see the *dinner;* and the gentlemen, who have the management of the place, showed me all about it. There are about *three thousand* persons fed here; and, if they were not thus fed, they must *either die*, or *thieve* or *rob;* or more properly *take by force;* for, in such a case, the words *theft* or *robbery* do not, according to the just laws of England, apply to the act; though they do apply, and, I hope, always will apply, in England.

I saw this "*dinner.*" In one long room, there were about 500 women, each with some potatoes in a bowl, mashed, as you mash them, to mix with *meal*, for your hogs. These people go to one end of the room, and, one at a time, get their mess. There are persons to put the potatoes into the bowl; which they do by taking the potatoes out of a tub, with a tin measure, holding about a quart, and putting the thing full in to the bowl, which is then carried away by the person who is to eat it; and all these persons are, as they eat, *standing up* in the room, as thick as they can stand. Each, as soon as the mess is eaten, goes away; and, as there is room made, others come in; and there were about three hundred then waiting in the yard to take their turn.

There were about a hundred little girls in a *school*, and about as many boys in another, neither had shoes or stockings, and the boys had *no shirts*. Their faces were pale, the whole hundred not having so much red as your little round-faced chap that was set to keep the birds away from the cabbage seed in Dodman's field. Yes, Marshall, that little chap, with his satchel full of bread and cheese or bacon; he was at the *proper school!* He and Tom Deadman and little Barratt will make strong and able men like their fathers; will live well, and be well clothed; and will be respected like their fathers, and be happy in that state of life in which it has pleased God to place them; and will not, I hope, listen to any practical man, who would persuade them, that to starve in rags, in this world, has a tendency to give them a crown of glory in the next.

In another place I saw a great crowd of women sitting and doing nothing, each with a *baby* in her arms. They were sitting in rows, waiting, I believe, for their messes. Some of them were young and naturally handsome; but made ugly by starvation, rags, and dirt. It was one mass of rags; and, not what *you* call rags; not rags such as you see on the beggars or gipsies that go to hopping at Farnham; but far worse than any that you ever saw tied round a stake to frighten the birds from our wheat and our peas; far worse than the Kentish people and South Hampshire people put up on a *scarecrow* to keep the birds from their cherries. And this is the condition, Marshall, to which the Scotch *feelosofer* vagabonds wish to persuade the Parliament to reduce the wives and the daughters of the working people of England! while they talk of *educating* you all, at the same time! Ah! Marshall, these vagabonds want to give you *books*, and to take away the *bread and meat* for themselves.

In another place I saw the most painful sight of all: *women*, with heavy hammers, *cracking stones* into very small pieces, to *make walks in gentlemen's gardens!* These women were as ragged as the rest; and the sight of them and their work, and the thoughts accompanying these, would have sunk the heart in your body, as they did mine. And are the women and girls of England to be brought to this state? Would not every man in Normandy suffer every drop of blood to be let out of his body rather than see your sisters and daughters and mothers and wives brought to this state? If I were not *sure* that Tom Farr would perish himself rather than see his sister brought to this, he should not live under my roof a moment longer. And what, then, of his good and industrious and kind and tender mother! The bare thought would drive him mad! Yet, Marshall, it is my duty to tell you, that the half-drunk and half-mad and greedy and crawling Scottish vagabonds, whose counsels have beggared the Scotch working people, are endeavouring to persuade the Parliament to bring your wives, mothers, sisters, and daughters into this very state! Be on your guard, therefore; be ready to perform *your duty* to prevent the success of these crawling villains, who hope to get rewarded for their schemes for making you work for 6d. a day, and for putting your wages into the pockets of the landlords. When I get back we will have a *meeting* at Guildford to petition the king and Parliament on the subject; to this meeting you must all come; for, though the law does not give you the right of *voting*, it always gives you the right of *petitioning;* and as I shall hereafter show you, it gives you *a right* to *parish relief* in case you be *unable* to *earn* a sufficiency to keep you in a proper manner. This is as much your *birthright* as is the lord of the manor's right to his estate; and of this we will convince the crawling and greedy vagabonds before we have done. It is our duty, too, to exert this right to endeavour to better the lot of our suffering fellow-subjects in Ireland. Mr. Dean will tell you, that I have always set my face against the ill-treatment of Irish people who go to get work in England. Their own food is sent away from them to England, for the benefit of their landlords; we receive the food, and it is monstrous injustice in us to frown upon them, if they come and offer their labour in exchange for a part of that very food which they themselves have raised.

*   *   *   *   *

I have not time to write any thing more to you now. I will, in future letters, tell you the *causes* of all this misery, and you will want nothing more to make you all resolve to use all the lawful means in your power to prevent it from falling on yourselves.

I am,

Your master and friend,

WM. COBBETT.

Cobbett's fame as a champion of the Irish people in Parliament and his alliance with the Irish Catholic Members on the floor of the House of Commons, meant that he was in constant demand as a speaker throughout his visit to Ireland. By now seventy-one years old, his two years in Parliament with their long late-night sittings were telling on his health. Perhaps it was his conviction that he was one of the few men who had the honesty and the ability to publish the truth about the Irish problem, perhaps it was the unexpected enthusiasm and gratitude with which he was greeted in Ireland, whatever it was, he found all his old energy and health restored. After his first speech in Dublin, he was heard by a reporter to say laughingly as he stepped off the balcony, 'I am as young a man as ever I was'. In the ten days he spent in Dublin, he gave three important lectures to packed audiences in the Fishamble Theatre on three consecutive nights, and received and replied to a number of 'elegantly written' addresses of welcome. Indeed, so great were the demands on his time that he felt obliged to insert the following notice in his paper of October 4th.

69

TO CORRESPONDENTS

I BEG, that, until my return to England, no one will give himself the trouble to write to me, on any subject whatsoever. A man cannot do more than one thing well at one time. I have quite enough to do here; and I will never, till I am again in England, open any letter that shall come to me from England. Some inconvenience may arise from this, and possibly some injury; but these I must submit to. At any rate, such is my determination.

It will be remembered that for years Cobbett had been crying out against the monstrous injustice of allowing the people of Ireland to live in destitution when quantities of food were being sent out of the country to enrich the profligate absentee landowners of the great Irish estates. Those of his readers who might have dismissed Cobbett's furious outbursts as wild exaggerations would surely have had to revise their opinions after reading the two next letters. Always more at home in the country than in the town, he was now speaking with a knowledge and authority that was difficult to challenge.

A word should be said here in explanation of Cobbett's constant references to the 'Scotch villains'. His dislike sprang from his abhorrence of the economic and social theories then in vogue – those of Adam Smith, eulogist of mass-production; those of Malthus, gloomy prophet of the doctrine of surplus population and advocate of sexual abstinence for the poor; and those of the 'Scotch vagabond' Brougham, Lord Chancellor, and leading proponent of the New Poor Laws. Not all the modern doctrines Cobbett abhorred, notably those of Bentham, James Mill and the Utilitarian School could properly be attributed to those whom Cobbett damned as 'Scotch feelosophers'; but he was right in ascribing to Scotland, and to the *Edinburgh Review* in particular, the source of the new climate of opinion which treated the working people as abstractions, as mere units of production, rather than as people with flesh and blood, emotions and desires, no different from those of the philosophers who wrote about them.

LETTER 3

City of Kilkenny.
1 *Oct.* 1834

MARSHALL,

From Dublin to this city is about 70 English miles. Very fine land all the way, except in very few places, and there the land is better than the greater part of the inclosed land in our part of Surrey; and, as to our *commons*, these people could not be made to believe, that there is any land so poor in the world; and yet I shall have to tell you presently, that those who do the work on this fine land, are in a state of poverty the most complete. When I get home, I will put INTO A LITTLE BOOK a full account of all that I see here. I only tell you in these letters, of such things as you can well understand; such things as will enable you to judge of the real state of the working people in this fine country; such things as will serve to show you what the Scotch, crawling vagabonds are endeavouring to persuade the Parliament to make you and your children submit to; giving you to understand, at the same time, that the *Scotch nation*, who are as good people as any in the world, detest and abhor these vagabonds as much as I do.

In coming from Dublin, I came through a horse-fair in a little town. I should think that there were two thousand horses; they were none of them what we call *large* horses; but, there was not a *poor* one amongst them all; and I have not seen a *poor* horse, colt, cow, ox, steer, heifer, sheep, hog, pig, goose, or turkey, or fowl, since I came into the country; *man* and *woman*, and *working* man and woman, are the only animals that suffer here from hunger and cold.

In this city of Kilkenny (which is the capital of a county of the same name), which is beautifully situated on a fine river, and which contains more than twenty thousand people, there are two societies for *assisting the poor*, one called the *charitable*, the other the *benevolent*. These societies make collections of money to relieve the poor; but, so great is the number of these poor, so low the wages, so great and

71

horrible the want, that these societies have been obliged to refuse all assistance to such as are *able to beg;* and also, to all persons who are *able to get one meal in* 24 *hours, of the very worst sort of potatoes, which they call* "Lumpers." And mind, Marshall, I have the proof of these facts under the assurance of gentlemen of the city, and under the hands of the managers of these very societies. And, Marshall, I beg you all to mind what I say, this is the state to which, it is my firm belief, all of you and your children will come, if you do not do your duty by petitioning the Parliament to protect you. If the *poor-laws* of England be put down, this is the state to which you must come; and about that great matter I will tell you another time; so that you and all of you may understand what to do.

I told you, in my first letter, that I saw fine *Swedish Turnips* and *Mangel-Wurzel.* They belonged to a rich gentleman, who got some of my seed. I have not seen another piece of either in the country! Having seen the people in the *cities,* I went, yesterday, to see them *in the country;* and I saw the state of both *labourers* and *farmers.* There was one village with about as many houses as there are in the village of Ash, about 70 or 80 perhaps, the scattered ones and all. The places, which I *call* houses, were, in general from ten to twelve feet square; the walls made of rough stone and mud, whited over, and about nine feet high; no ceiling; rough rafters covered with old rotten black thatch; in some a glass window the size of your hat, in two or four little panes; in others no window at all; but a hole or two holes in the wall; about a foot long, and four or five inches wide; the floor nothing but the bare earth; no chimney, but a hole at one end of the roof to let out the smoke, arising from a fire made against the wall of that end of this miserable shed; this hole is sometimes surrounded by a few stones put on that part of the roof a foot or two high; generally it is not, and in cold weather, the poor, ragged, half-naked creatures *stop up the hole to keep in the smoke to keep them from perishing with cold!* The fuel is *peat,* just such as that dug out of our moors, and never a stick of wood; and the people get the big *dead weeds* to light their fires and to

72

boil their potatoes. One of these places costs the landowner about *four pounds* to build it, and the poor creatures pay from *thirty shillings* to *two pounds* a year rent for them, without any garden, without an inch of land, without any place for even a *privy*, WOMEN as well as men must go to the *dung-heap before the door*, and the former are exposed to that which your wife, or any woman of Normandy, would die at the thought of! And, Marshall, this is the state to which the crawling and greedy Scotch vagabonds would fain have the Parliament reduce you, in order to enrich the land-owners, hoping to get from them rewards for their schemes. But, will our member of Parliament, Mr. Leech, listen to such damnable advice? No; and it is our bounden duty to support him in his opposition to all such hard-hearted schemes.

As to the *goods* in the hole, there are, an *iron pot*, a *rough table*, or a *board laid across two piles of stones*, seats of stones, or of boards laid from one stone to another; and that is all the stock of goods, except a *dish*, of which I shall speak presently. Every hole has a pig; the pig eats with the family, and generally sleeps in the same place. The potatoes are taken up and turned out into a great *dish*, which dish is a shallow basket made of oziers with the bark on. The family squat round this basket and take out the potatoes with their hands; the pig stands and is helped by some one, and sometimes he eats out of the pot. He goes in and out and about the hole, like one of the family; the family sleep, huddled up together, on dead weeds or a little straw in one corner of the hole, and the pig, on a similar bed in another corner. The pig is the person of most consequence; he is sold to *pay the rent*: if he fail, the family are turned out into the naked air to perish, which has been the case in many thousands of instances, there being *no poor-law* here to save their lives.

I must speak to you about *the farmers* in my next letter. In the meanwhile pay great attention to what I have said here; and all of you make up your minds to be brought into this state, or *resolve* to do your duty in the manner that I have before described. Men are brought into this state by *little* and *little*, until at last they cannot help themselves. Mind this! And attend, all of you, to the advice of

Your master and friend,

WM. COBBETT.

LETTER 4

Waterford,
6 *Oct.* 1834

MARSHALL,

I broke off my last letter in telling you, that I would tell you about the *farmers* another time. There are *some* large farmers, and these have *barns* and thrashing-machines; but the greater number have from 5 acres of land to 40 perhaps. *Our acre* is about three quarters of an *Irish acre;* but I speak of *our acre.* Where there are barns, they are of *stone.* The ground of all this kingdom seems to be upon beds of stone, and great part *lime-stone;* so that all buildings are of these, stone and mortar; and the *fences,* where there are any, are of stone. The *farmers* in general have *no barns.* They put their sheaves into little cocks and seldom thatch them; and they do the same with the hay. They beat out the corn (wheat, &c.) in *their miserable houses,* and winnow it by the wind, on cloths, having no vans to do it with. They then put it into bags holding about six of our bushels, which are lifted on a *car* (a sort of *bed* of a cart without head or tail or sides, which, when wanted to carry potatoes or apples, are made of *oziers*), and carry it and sell it to the corn-dealers, who send almost all of it to England. The *farmer* and his family are all in half nakedness or rags; their lot is little better than the mere labourers. They raise wheat and barley and oats and butter and pork in great abundance; but never do they *taste* any of either, except, perchance, a small part of the meal of the oats. Potatoes are their sole food. I wish the farmers of our parish could see one that I saw in the fine county of Kilkenny. His dress was a mere bundle of rags, tied round his body with a band of straw; his legs and feet bare, no shirt, and his head covered with a rag, such as you would rip out of the inside of an old *cart-saddle.* The landlord generally lets his great estate to some *one man,* who lets it out in littles; and this *one man*

74

takes *all* from the wretched farmer. Some of the farmers in England *grumble* at the *poor-rates*. Well, there are *no poor-rates here!* Let them come here then, and lead the life of these farmers! They will soon find that there is something worse than poor-rates! And if the Scotch vagabonds, of whom I have spoken so often, should succeed in their schemes, you may tell the farmers of our parish, that they will be *in this very state;* that their wives will have no hats, bonnets, or caps; but must, in wet weather, *have a wad of straw tied upon their heads!* Mrs. West and Mrs. Faggotten and Mrs. Heathorn would look so nice, naked up to the knees, some rags tied round their middle, no smock, and their heads covered with a wad of straw! And this will be their lot, if ever the poor-rates be abolished in England; as the Scotch villains (who have *beggared the industrious people of their own country*) are endeavouring to prevail on the Parliament to abolish them in England.

Marshall, I have now been over about 180 miles in Ireland, in the several counties of Dublin, Wicklow, Kildare, Carlow, Kilkenny and Waterford. I have, in former years, been in every county of England, and across every county more than one way. I have been through the finest parts of Scotland. I have lived in the finest parts of the United States of America. And here I am to declare to all the world, that I never passed over any 50 miles, in my life, any 50 *unbroken miles*, of land so good on an average during the whole way, as the average of these 180 miles. Perhaps there are parts, *patches*, of England better than this land; but take England, one with the other, it is nothing like so good as this; and yet here are these starving people! And this is only because they have *no law* to give them their due share of the fruits of their labour!

In coming from Kilkenny to Waterford, I and my friend, (Mr. O'Higgins), in a post-chaise, came through a little town called Mullinavat, where there was a fair for *cattle* and *fat hogs* and *apples*. There might be 4,000 people; there were about 7 acres of ground covered with cattle (mostly fat), and all over the street of the town there were about THREE THOUSAND BEAUTIFUL FAT HOGS, lying all over the road and the streets; and our chaise was *actually stopped and blocked up by fat hogs;* and we were obliged to stop till the civil and kind people could get them out of our way! There was a sight to be seen by me, who had never seen thirty such hogs together in the course of my life, these hogs weighing from *ten* to *thirty scores* each! Ah! but there arose out of this fine sight reflections that made my blood boil; that the far greater part of those who had bred and fatted these hogs were never to taste one morsel of them, no not even the offal, and had lived *worse* than the hogs, not daring to taste any part of the *meal* used in the fatting of the hogs! The hogs are to be killed, dried or tubbed, and sent out of the country to be sold for money to be *paid* to *the landowners,* who spend it in London, Bath, Paris, Rome, or some other place of pleasure, while these poor creatures are raising all this food from the land, and are starving themselves. And this is what we shall come to *in England,* unless we call upon our member, Mr. Leech, to protect us.

I will tell you more about these *landowners* another time; but I will now, before I conclude this letter, give you *one fact,* which will enable you to judge of what would be the lot of the working men in England, if there were to be no *poor-rates.* There are here, as there are in England, several *sorts* of potatoes: some are called *minions,* others *apple-potatoes;* these are the *best.* Others are called *lumpers;* and these are the *worst.* When men or women are employed at 6d. a day and their *board,* to dig *minions* or *apple-potatoes,* they are not suffered to *taste them,* but are sent to another field to dig *lumpers* to eat; and this is called *boarding* them! That fact is enough: it is enough for you to know that THAT is what the Scotch vagabonds mean when they propose to bring you to "COARSER food": it is enough for you to know THAT to *rouse you all to a sense of your danger,* and to urge you to come to a *county-meeting* and do your duty like men, true to your country and true to the King and to the laws of England.

I hope that all of you are well; and that not a man of you will ever again suffer a potato to grow in your gardens, or be brought into your houses; and if any one bring a potato into my house, except to *stuff a fat goose*, or a *fat sucking pig*, Mr. Dean has my order to *discharge that person directly*. You have peas and beans of all sorts for summer; carrots, parsnips, beets for winter; white cabbages *all the year through;* the best of bread, bacon, and puddings always; and if you still hanker after that accursed root without which Ireland could not have been brought to its present state, and which has *banished bread* from the labourer's house here; if you still hanker after this "COARSER food," you shall go elsewhere to get it; for you shall not have it in the service (in house or out of house) of

Your master and friend,

WM. COBBETT.

From Kilkenny and Waterford where Cobbett received and answered addresses from the citizens of both towns, Cobbett travelled through the country to Cork. When reading the next letters one is staggered by the sheer physical energy of a man of his age who, after enduring the long drives over the rough roads of the time, was able to set down his impressions in faultless prose, and find the courage to address huge crowds on the subject of Poor Laws which he knew would be unpopular as contrary to the expressed opinions of their darling and idol, Daniel O'Connell. He did all this and more too. While he was in Ireland, Cobbett wrote for each issue of his weekly Political Register, not only one of his Letters to Marshall, but other articles on matters of current concern. He was witty on the fire which destroyed the House of Commons while he was away, angry over the sum of twenty million pounds which had been granted by the Exchequer to rich plantation-owners to compensate them for the emancipation of their slaves, and admonitory over the terrible effects the New Poor Law Act would have on the English labouring classes. It was no idle promise he made immediately after his election to Parliament in 1832: 'Now, I belong to the people of Oldham'.

LETTER 5

Cork,
17 *Oct.* 1834

MARSHALL,

Since the date of my last letter I have been in the City of
Kilkenny, and have, in a long speech, urged the justice and
necessity of *poor-laws*, such as we have always had in
England. In another letter, when I get more time, I will
tell you how our poor-laws came to be, and I will prove to
you, that, in case of need, you have *as clear a right to relief
out of my farm, as I have to my cows or my corn, or as Mr.
Woodruffe has to the land or the timber.* Our rights are very
clear; but not more clear than *yours* are. At present I must
speak to you of some little part of what I have recently seen
and heard. When I get back to Normandy, I shall make *a
book*, relating to every thing about this country.

From Kilkenny I came to Clonmell, the capital of the
county of Tipperary, which is deemed one of the finest in
Ireland. The land, in this distance of about 35 English
miles, is very fine, except in a few places. But, only four
turnip fields all the way. The harvest was here *all got in.* But,
the grass! The fine grass fields covered with herds of fine
cattle; fine oxen; fine cows; fine sheep; all seemed fat; and
to every miserable thing *called a house*, a fine hog, so white,
clean, and fat, so unlike the poor souls who had reared it
up and fatted it, and who were destined never to taste one
morsel of it; no, not so much as the offal.

At the town of Clonmell, I went to see one of the places
where they kill and salt hogs to send to England. In *this one
town*, they kill every year, for this purpose, about *sixty thousand hogs*, weighing from *eight score* to *twenty score*. Every
ounce of this meat is sent out of Ireland, while the poor
half-naked creatures, who raise it with such care, are compelled to live on the *lumpers*, which are such bad potatoes,
that the hogs will not thrive on them, and will not touch
them, if they can get other potatoes. The *rooks*, which eat
the good potatoes, will not eat these, though they be starving. And, yet, this is the stuff *that the working people* are fed
on. There are about *eighty thousand firkins of butter*, and,

78

perhaps, *a hundred thousand quarters of wheat*, and more of *oats*, sent away out of this one town; while those who raise it all by their labour, live upon *lumpers!* "How," you will ask, "are the *millions* of working people made to *submit* to this?" I will tell you, when I get back to the Parliament House, or to a county meeting at Guildford. It will be better to say it *there* than here!

From Clonmell we came to Fermoy, on Saturday, the 11 instant. Fine land; a fine country; flocks of turkeys all along the way; cattle, sheep, hogs, as before; and the people, the working people, equally miserable as before. Here is a fine view, and beautiful meadows, compared to which the meadows at Farnham are not worth naming. From one side of this valley there rises up a long and most beautiful chain (miles in length) of gently sloping hills, and on those hills and on their sides, corn-fields and grass-fields are interspersed with woods and groves. But, standing on the bridge, and viewing this scene, my *eyes were blasted* by the sight of three BARRACKS for *foot, horse*, and *artillery;* buildings surpassing in extent all the palaces that I ever saw; elegant and costly as palaces; buildings containing, they say, three thousand windows and capable of lodging forty thousand men! "Good God!" say you, "what can all this BE FOR?" I will tell you, Marshall, when I get to the county meeting at Guildford, to which you must all come. "But," you will say, "do these *soldiers* live upon *lumpers* too?" Marshall, do not *ask me* any more questions about this matter. Ask Mr. Dean; he can tell you all about it.

But, now, Marshall, I am coming *nearer home;* and I beg you all to pay great attention to what I am going to say. You will think it strange, that all this food should be sent out of the country, and that the people should *get nothing back* for it. You will think, that we must send them *clothes* and *household goods* and *tea* and *sugar* and *soap* in return for the hogs and other things. To the *rich* we do; and to the *barracks;* but, the millions of working people have only rags for parts of their bodies, and they have neither goods nor tea nor sugar nor plate nor knife nor fork nor tea-kettle nor cup nor saucer.

79

The case is this: the owners of all the great estates *live in England or in France or in Italy.* The *rents are sent to them;* and, as there are *no poor-rates,* they get all the produce of the land from the miserable farmer, except just enough to keep him alive. They *spend these rents out of Ireland;* so that the working people here, who might eat meat three times a day, are compelled to live upon *lumpers!* And, be you assured, that this would be the lot of the English working people, if the Scotch vagabonds could succeed in their projects for sweeping away our poor-laws. If that were done, the English farmers would be a set of beggarly slaves, the landlords would take so much from them, that they would be able to give the labourers not more than 6d. a day, and you would all be living in hovels without chimneys, and be eating with the pigs, that you would be rearing and fatting for somebody else to eat! And, are you to *come to this?* I would rather see you all perish, and perish along with you!

But, Marshall, mind me well. You know, that, at Pepperharrow (only about four miles from your cottage) there lives LORD MIDDLETON. You know that he was a long while Lord-Lieutenant of our county. Now, Marshall, HE is one of the GREAT LANDOWNERS OF IRELAND. His real name is BRODERICK. He is the owner of a *town* called *Middleton,* half as big as Guildford. He is the owner of the lands for many miles round, and, it is supposed, that he draws, *yearly, from twenty-five to thirty thousand pounds from this estate!*

I came here to see things with my own eyes; and, I have, *to-day,* been to see this BRODERICK's estate, which begins at about sixteen miles from this City of Cork; and the land of this sixteen miles, taking in two miles on each side of the road, the finest that you can possibly imagine. Ah! but, how did I find the *working people* upon this land of this Broderick? That is the question for you to ask, and for me to answer.

I went to a sort of hamlet near to the town of Middleton. It contained about 40 or 50 hovels. I went into several of them, and took down the names of the occupiers. They all consisted of mud-walls, with a covering of rafters and straw. None of them so good as the place where you keep your little horse. I took a particular account of the first that I went into. It was 21 feet long and 9 feet wide. The floor, the bare ground. No fire-place, no chimney, the fire (made of potato-haulm) made on one side against the wall, and the smoke going out of a hole in the roof. No table, no chair: I sat to write upon a block of wood. Some stones for seats. No goods but *a pot*, and a shallow tub, for the pig and the family both to eat out of. There was one window, 9 inches by 5, and the glass broken half out. There was a mud-wall about 4 feet high to separate off the end of the shed for the family to sleep, lest the hog should kill and eat the little children when the father and mother were both out, and when the hog was shut in; and it happened some time ago that a poor mother, being ill on her straw, unable to move, and having her baby dead beside her, *had its head eaten off by a hog before her own eyes!* No bed: no mattress; some large flat stones laid on other stones, to keep the bodies from the damp ground; some dirty straw and a bundle of rags were all the bedding. The man's name was Owen Gumbleton. *Five small children;* the mother, about thirty, naturally handsome, but worn into half-ugliness by hunger and filth; she had no shoes or stockings, no shift, a mere rag over her body and down to her knees. The man BUILT THIS PLACE HIMSELF, and yet he has to pay a *pound a year* for it with perhaps a rod of ground! Others, 25s. a year. *All built their own hovels*, and yet have to pay this rent. All the hogs were in the hovels today, it being coldish and squally; and then, you know, hogs like cover. Gumbleton's hog was lying in the room; and in another hovel there was a fine large hog that had taken his bed close by the fire. There is a nasty dunghill (no privy) to each hovel. The dung that the hog makes *in the hovel* is carefully put into a heap by itself, as being the most precious. This dung and the pig are the main things to raise the rent and to get fuel with. The poor creatures sometimes *keep the dung in the hovel*, when their hard-hearted tyrants will not suffer them to let it be at the door! So there they are, in a far worse state, Marshall, than any hog that you ever had in your life.

Lord Middleton may say, that HE is not the *landlord* of

these wretched people. Ah! but his *tenant*, his *middleman*, is their landlord, and Lord Middleton gets the *more rent from him*, by enabling him to let these holes in this manner. If I were to give Mr Dean a shilling a week to squeeze you down to twelve shillings a week, who would you think was most to blame, me or Mr. Dean?

Now, Marshall, pray remember that this horrible state of things never could take place if the Irish people had those poor-laws, which the Scotch Vagabonds would advise the Parliament to take from us. For then THE LAW would compel those who have the estates to pay sufficiently those without whose labour the land is worth nothing at all.

And even without *poor-rates*, the people never could have been brought to this pass without the ever-damned *potatoes!* People CAN keep life in them by the means of this nasty, filthy, *hog-feed;* and the tyrants make them do it, and have thus reduced them to the state of hogs, and worse than that of hogs.

I repeat to you, therefore, that if any person bring a potato into my house, for any purpose whatever, Mr. Dean is hereby authorized and directed to discharge that person. And, Marshall, while I will give you, or any man, and all the men, *in the tithing*, the finest cabbage, carrot, parsnip, beet, and any other seed, and my corn to plant, I will *never again give constant employment to any man* in whose garden I shall see potatoes planted. I have no right to dictate to you what you shall plant, but I have a right to employ my money as I please, and it is both my pleasure and my duty to discourage in every way that I can the cultivation of this damned root, being convinced that it has done more harm to mankind than the sword and the pestilence united.

I am very much pleased to hear from Mr. Dean that you are all sober and dutiful, and that you have made the farm so clean; and hoping that all of you and your wives, children and relations, are well, I am,

Your master and friend,
WM. COBBETT.

LETTER 6

Castle Comfort,
Abington, Co. Limerick,
25 Oct. 1834

MARSHALL,

Since I wrote to you from Cork, I have been over a hundred more miles of this country. There is no *sandy* ground here, and no *chalk*. It is all *loam* and *rocky stone*, and great part of this stone is *lime-stone* of a very dark blue colour. In some parts the stone is near to the top of the ground, and in others, quite at the top, so that the ground cannot be ploughed. But, even here, the grass is very fine between the rocky stones, and as good for sheep as our *downs* are. There are few *hills*, compared with our part of England: some about as high as those that rise up in our neighbourhood; and these they call "Mountains"; but, the greater part of those that I have seen are covered with grass to their very tops; and have hundreds of cattle fatting on their sides, and the very tips.

I came, yesterday, along a country about ten English miles long, all the richest land that can possibly be. On the two sides of this road, and on those of its continuation for ten miles farther, there are about a hundred and fifty thousand acres of land; a bed of rich loam from 6 to 8 feet deep, and without a single *water-furrow* being wanted in the whole of it; and yet, on the whole of this tract, which is worth more than all the land in the county of Surrey, there is not one field of turnips, mangel-wurzel, or cabbages. The land is not tilled a tenth part so well as it might be. If *we* had it, it would be all a garden; and it is not the fault of the farmers and working people; but of the LAWS, which suffer the landlords to take away and send into other countries all the meat and the corn, and compel the miserable farmers and working people to live on potatoes. But, all this matter I shall make clear to you all in a BOOK that I shall make when I get back to Normandy, or before.

In my last letter I told you about the poor souls on Lord Middleton's estate; and, I shall tell you, that his poor creatures are looked upon as being the *best treated* of any in the

83

country. Well, then, Marshall, if that be the *best of it*, you may guess *what is the worst!* No; you cannot guess: and God forbid, that the Scotch or the English place-hunting and tax-eating miscreants should ever be able to persuade the Parliament to *attempt* to reduce the people of Surrey to such a state as to enable them to *guess* at horrors such as I have beheld since I last wrote to you.

I have been TO SEE the people on the estates of several great swaggering fellows, who are called "*noblemen*," and who live in England and spend there, or in France or in Italy, the money that the Irish corn and meat sell for. I have seen a few hundreds of Irish FARMERS, now, Marshall, and have taken down their names, and a correct account of all about them. Marshall, you call yourself a *poor man;* and, with 8 children, only one of whom can constantly earn his living, you cannot be otherwise; but, I solemnly declare to you, that I have seen no *Irish farmer*, who lives in a manner any thing like equal to the manner in which you live. At the house of one (who pays as much rent as Farmer Horne) there was a boy six years old (stabbling about on the dirt-floor, in the urine of the pig) naked all but a rag round his middle, and we judged, some of us, that this rag might weigh 4 ounces, and, others, that it might weigh 6 ounces. This was a "*farmer's son*"! But this farmer *pays no poor-rates* as Farmer Horne does! And this farmer pays a working man only 6d. a day, while Farmer Horne is obliged to pay him 2s. Ah! but the LANDLORD here takes away from the Irish farmer rent, poor-rates, wages, and all, and thus reduces the whole to beggary. And this, Marshall, is precisely what a FAMOUS SCOTCH VAGABOND, of whom I will tell you more another time, is endeavouring to cause to take place in England. Look sharp, then, and especially the FARMERS look sharp; be prepared to use, and, in good earnest, all the lawful means in your power, to uphold the laws of England, those just laws, which were obtained by the good sense and resolution and best blood of our virtuous and wise and just and resolute forefathers.

In one street in the outskirts of the city of Limerick (which is made a *fine city* by the trade of sending away

84

meat and butter and corn out of Ireland), I saw more misery than any man could have believed existed in the whole world. Men sleeping in the same wisp of dirty straw, or weeds, with their mothers, sisters, and aunts; and compelled to do this, or perish; two or three families in one room, that is to say, a miserable hole 10 feet by 8 or 9; and husbands, wives, sons, daughters, all huddled together, paying 6d. or 8d. or 10d. a week for *the room;* and the rent paid to a *"nobleman"* in England! Here I saw one woman with a baby in her arms, both nearly naked. The poor mother's body was naked from the middle of her thighs downwards; and to hide *her bosom,* she caught up a dirty piece of old sack; she hung down her face (naturally very pretty); when she lifted it up, the tears were streaming down her cheeks. Her husband, who had just got better after illness, was out of work. She had two other children quite naked, and covered up in some dirty hay, in one corner of the room! At a place in the country, I went to the dwelling of a widower, who is 60 years of age, and who has five children, all *very nearly stark naked.* The eldest girl, who is *fifteen years of age,* had on a sort of apron to hide the middle part of her body before; and that was all she had. She hid herself, as well as she could, behind, or at the end of, an old broken cupboard; and she held up her two arms and hands to hide her breasts! This man *pays* 30s. *rent* for an acre of the poorest land! And, am I to live to see the working people of Guildford and Godalming, and of my native town of Farnham, *brought to this state!* Yet, Marshall, mind what I say; to this state they will be brought, if they do not do every thing that the law allows them to do to prevent it. Mind, Marshall, I have *witnesses* to the truth of all the horrid facts that I state; and, I am ready to bring *proof* of these facts before a committee of the House of Commons. I have the *names* of scores of FARMERS, and an account of thousands, who *never taste* either *meat* or *bread!* Yet, they *do not pay poor-rates!*

Marshall, you know that there is a great swaggering fellow, in Sussex, that they call "the EARL OF EGREMONT." I will give you an account of his "FARMERS" another time.

Tell Farmer Horne, that I say, he ought to read these letters to his congregation, and to read to them those parts of the Bible which relate to the duties of the rich towards the poor. Be sure to get some of them to Purbright, and to all the parishes round about. Let them all see what the Scotch and English tax-eating vagabonds wish to persuade the Parliament to bring them to; and let them all be ready to come to a county meeting when I get back. Mr. Dean will read to you the account of the great kindness of the Irish people to me. *"God bless you and your countrymen!"* I have heard from hundreds of thousands of voices, since I came to Ireland; and, if we do not do our best, in every legal way that we can act, to better the lot of this good and kind and most cruelly suffering prople, we shall deserve to be reduced to their horrible state; our hard-heartedness, or cowardice, will merit suffering even greater than those which they have to endure.

I begin to look towards Normandy again. I never see a *"farmhouse"* here, without thinking how happy one of these "farmers" (who pay no *poor-rates*) would be, if he had a sleeping-place as good as that which you and Tom Farr made for our *bull!* You thought, that it would not be *"decent"* without *paving!* I declare to God that I have not seen a foot of square pavement in a farm-house in Ireland; and yet these farmers are not *"oppressed* by *poor-rates"!* I once thought of bringing Sam Riddle with me. I wish I had, and then sent him down to his own home, in Sussex, to tell the farmers there what he had seen. He would have been able to tell them the consequence of getting relieved from poor-rates; and to relate to them *how* it was, that poor-rates prevented the landlords from swallowing up poor-rates and wages along with the rents, and of reducing farmers as well as labourers to potatoes and salt.

Hoping that you all keep sober and very obedient to Mr. Dean, and that you will have every thing in nice order against my return, I remain in excellent health, and with sincere wishes for the health of you all,

Your master and friend,

Wm. COBBETT.

From Cork Cobbett returned to Dublin and the last three letters take on a different tone. Now his task is to present his general conclusions. He had expressed many of these views before, for one must remember that the conditions of the working classes in England had been steadily deteriorating since the beginning of the century. Cobbett now feared that that deterioration, exacerbated by the New Poor Laws and the failure of the Reformed Parliament to champion the labouring people, might bring the English labourer down to the level of the Irish. He was already appalled by the living conditions of the English poor. What he learnt in Ireland was that those conditions could be forced down to depths he had never imagined to be possible.

In his book 'Cobbett's Sermons' published in 1822, he had expounded at some length his interpretation of the laws of God: in the seventh and eighth letters of November 4th and 10th he can repeat these views more simply and more effectively with the fearful scenes in Ireland fresh in his readers' minds. In the last letter of November 15th, defending but not condoning the English rioters who were at this time setting fire to ricks and barns, he again expresses views not very different from the comments he had made on earlier rioting in England when widespread distress had provoked similar disturbances. But never before had he spelt out in such unequivocal terms his views on private property. The scenes he had witnessed in Ireland led him to break new ground, and the book 'Legacy to Labourers' which he sketches out in the last letter will be referred to in some detail in Part III.

LETTER 7

Dublin,
4 November, 1834

MARSHALL,

I dare say that my letters have made you stare; but, staring is not all that they ought to make you do: they ought to make you think about how you would like to have a naked wife and children; how you would like to have no

87

shoes or stockings, or shirt, and the mud spewing up between your toes when you come down the road to your work of a morning. They ought to make you think about what you shall *do, all of you,* to prevent this state of starvation, nakedness, and filth, from coming upon you. Do not think that it is IMPOSSIBLE that it ever should come upon you. Do not think this; for there is no *reason* for your thinking it. The countries are very close to one another. The county of Cork is but a very little way from Somersetshire. I am not so far from you now as I should be if I were at Morpeth in the county of Northumberland. The same Ministers and the same Parliament who keep this people in this state, after having got them into it, are the same Ministers and same Parliament who have the power of making laws, and of employing soldiers and policemen in England. This miserable people have been brought to this state by little and little, and for want of beginning in time to *do the things which they ought to have done in their own defence;* to make use of the faculties which God has given them; that is to say, in legally and constitutionally, and according to the good custom of our wise and brave forefathers petitioning the King and the Parliament, and otherwise legally doing that, which the laws of our country bid us do, sanctioned as those laws are by the laws of God.

Marshall, I told you that you had as much *right,* as clear a legal right to parish relief; that you had as much right to relief out of the produce of my farm, in case of necessity; in case of illness in your family; in case of inability in yourself to work; or in case of your being unable to get work. I told you that, in either of these cases, you had as clear a legal right to relief out of the produce of my farm, as I had to the rest of the produce; or as Mr. Woodruffe had to his rent. To *prove* this to you, and to all of you, will require one long letter; and I have not time to write that now; but I will mention a few things just to prepare the way for giving you such proof.

You will observe, Marshall, that I shall attempt to say nothing about the matter which I cannot prove to be according to the *laws of England;* those laws which we owe

88

to our wise and resolute forefathers. I could tell you (and Farmer Horne ought to tell his congregation), that the Holy Bible, which you know, Marshall, is the word of God, commands, from one end of it to the other, that the working man shall receive his full hire; that provision shall always be made for those who are too poor to help themselves; that the widow, the fatherless, and the stranger, shall be taken care of, and that all manner of curses shall fall upon the rich, if they do not take care of them. Farmer Horne should take care to read to his congregation those passages of the New Testament, in which our Saviour and his apostles warned the rich of the curses that shall alight upon them if they despise or neglect the poor. He ought to read to them the fifth chapter of St. James, which begins thus: "Go, you rich men, weep and howl for your miseries "that shall come upon you: the rust of your gold and silver "shall eat your flesh as it were *fire*. You have by fraud kept "back the hire of your labourers who have reaped down "your fields; and their cries have entered into the ears of the Lord." He should read to them the passage in the 15 chapter of Deuteronomy, which tells the farmer, that, when the labourer has served him faithfully for a length of time, and when he sends him away, not wanting him any more, he is not to send him away empty, either as to belly, back, or hands: he should read to them this: "When thou "sendest him away thou shalt not let him go empty: thou "shalt furnish him liberally out of thy flock, out of thy floor "and out of thy wine-press. Of that wherewith the Lord "thy God hath blessed thee, thou shalt give unto him."

Now, Marshall, this is the word of God; and it is the business of the parsons and of Farmer Horne to read these things to you and to me, that we may know our duty. It is my duty to give a good and faithful servant plenty of meat from my flock of sheep, or my drove of hogs; to give them plenty of flour or bread, coming from the wheat that shall be thrashed upon my floor. In the country where God promulgated his law, grapes grow naturally in the fields, and the climate is too hot for the keeping of beer. Therefore, they drank wine, as we drink beer; and as it was their duty to supply the labourer out of the wine-press, so it is our duty to supply him out of the mash-tub. Not a hint is here given about infamous potatoes and salt. The law of God forbids to muzzle the ox while he is treading out the corn. In those hot countries they make use of cattle to tread out the corn, the corn is so dry. It was, and, is, the custom of those countries, to employ oxen, or horses, to tread the corn out; and, in order that the farmers should be merciful and just, even to the animals that they employed, God commands, in the 25 chapter of Deuteronomy, "Thou shalt not "*muzzle* the ox when he treadeth out the corn"; that is to say, thou shalt not pinch him, thou shalt not take from him a share of that which he has caused to come. And what can be more just than this? For what would my farm be good for, and how would Mr. Woodruffe get any rent out of it, if it were not for the labour that you and the rest of you bestow upon it; and how are you to perform that labour, unless you have out of it a sufficiency to eat and to drink and to wear?

Such, then, is a specimen of the laws of God. The laws of England say, that nothing can be law of man, which is contrary to the laws of God. It is the very first principle of the laws of England; and this principle is laid down by all our great lawyers in all ages, that any rule, regulation, or call it what you will, which is contrary to the laws of God, cannot be law in England. Begging you to bear this in mind; begging those who can read it, to read it to those who cannot read, I shall conclude for the present, promising you that, in another letter, I will show you, that the laws which were left us by our forefathers, and which are the birthright of us all, are in perfect agreement with these laws of the King of kings and of the Ruler of the rulers of the earth.

Hoping that you are all well, and that you will not let me see a weed on the farm by the time that I get back; and in full confidence that no half-drunk and half-mad vagabond will be able to induce any body to do any thing that shall take away your shirts and your shoes and your stockings, make you live upon *lumpers*, and sleep upon hog dung, covered over with dirty straw: thus trusting, and trusting also to your own sense and own spirit, to make that lawful use of your rights, which will prevent so great a disgrace falling upon England,

I remain,
Your master and friend,
WM. COBBETT.

LETTER 8

Shangana Castle,
10 Nov. 1834

MARSHALL,

Since I wrote to you last I have learned that, when the charitable and most benevolent Catholic priests have contrived to collect a little money to give to poor creatures who are sick, and even in danger of dying; when the poor sick person gets a sixpence or a shilling in this way, intended to buy him some little comforting thing, the poor creature is frequently obliged to give the bit of money thus obtained to pay the rent of the place where he is, for fear of being flung into the street by the agent of the great lord to whom the house belongs! There are poor women, who, having got a few pence by begging from shopkeepers and other persons in the middle rank of life, purchase herrings and tobacco with the pence, then go to the country and *swap* these for potatoes; then come into the town, eat some of the potatoes, and sell the rest to pay the rent of the great English landlord. A Catholic priest has informed me that *dung* is constantly made in cellar-rooms, *under the bed* that the poor creatures lie on! The other day this Catholic priest (whose name I shall be ready to state to the House of Commons) informed me, that he had just been to visit a sick man on his death bed, expected every hour to die. He found an ass tied to the foot of the bed, which was laid on a frame of old rough boards; man, ass, pig, and family slept, and had the dung-heap, in the same room! In the country it is a common thing to see the farmer's cow sleeping in the *same room*, with the pig and the family, with a heap of dung, as you know there must be, Marshall, in such a case, every morning.

Marshall, I shall have a great deal more to say to you

91

another time; and a great deal more to say to the whole nation, in a little book; and still more to say to the Parliament when I shall meet it, on the subject of this condition of this kind and good people who inhabit the most fertile country upon the face of God's earth; who themselves, while they see the oxen, the hogs, the sheep, the butter, the corn, sent away out of their country in hundreds and thousands of ship-loads, never taste either meat or bread themselves; but see it all taken away from them, while they are reduced to live upon the very worst sort of potatoes and salt at the very best. I shall have a great deal more to say to you and our neighbours and to the nation and to the Parliament upon this subject; but, at present, I will point out to you what the law of God is upon this subject. I shall, in a short time, publish a *Bible for Poor Men;* but I will just show you here what God has said upon this subject, in one instance or two. You will bear in mind, Marshall, that it is the business of the parson to read the Bible to you and to me; that this is his principal business, and that he gets the tithes for this. You will also bear in mind, that there are Bible societies making great collections of money to distribute about the Bible amongst us. Therefore, into this Bible we ought to look, and see what God has told us to take for our guide in these matters; to see what he says shall be the fate of the oppressors of the poor.

In the tenth chapter of Isaiah, verses 1 and 2, we are told this: "Woe unto them that *decree unrighteous decrees,* and "that *write grievousness* which they have prescribed; to turn "aside the needy from judgment, and to take away the "RIGHT of the poor of my people, that the widows may be "their prey, and that they may *rob* the fatherless."

Now, Marshall, a decree is a law; and "writing grievousness," which has been "prescribed," means just such writings as are now coming from the Scotch vagabonds that I have so often mentioned; and it is very curious that the great object of these infamous writings is to take away the *right* of the poor, and to rob the widows and the fatherless!

But, Marshall, what is to be the end of those who put

92

forth unrighteous decrees; those who write *grievousness*, as the Scotch vagabonds are now writing; those who "turn aside the needy" when they apply for justice; those who strive to take away the RIGHT of the poor; those who are manifestly seeking to make the "widows a *prey*," and to "*rob* the fatherless"? What is to be the end of these Scotch vagabonds, and all those who assist and uphold them, let them be who they may? God says, that he will raise up a man to destroy them, to spread desolation amongst them, to make them feel the effects of his indignation at their conduct, to strip them of their property, and to "*tread them down like the mire of the streets.*" This is what God says shall be done to those who are the oppressors of the poor, or who try to oppress them.

In the fifth chapter of the prophet Amos, the oppressors of the poor are denounced in these words, in verses 11 and 12. "Forasmuch as your treading is upon the poor, and ye take from him burdens of wheat: ye have built houses of hewn stone, but ye shall not dwell in them; ye have planted pleasant vineyards, but ye shall not drink wine of them. For I know your manifold transgressions and your mighty sins: they afflict the just, they take a bribe, and they turn aside the poor in the gate *from their right.*" You see, Marshall, how all the prophets and all the apostles agree as to this matter. The villains, the Scotch vagabonds, are not, however, to profit from their villany in the end. "They take a *bribe.*" A bribe means money given to people to do wicked things; and here the word of God points directly at these Scotch vagabonds, for they are notoriously hired and paid "to turn aside the poor *from their right.*" But, Marshall, what is to be the fate of those who take bribes? In the book of Job, chapter xv, and verse 34, we are told, that "the congregation of hypocrites shall be desolate, and that FIRE shall consume the tabernacles of BRIBERY"! Now, Marshall, a *tabernacle* means a house in which people live. God has told us before that there shall be "woe unto those that take a bribe to turn aside the poor *from* their right"; and he here tells us, that the tabernacles, or houses, of the bribed villains shall be *consumed by fire.*

Now, Marshall, if we believe the Bible to be the word of God, as I hope we all do, this is what God says upon the subject; and this is what will assuredly come to pass, if these Scotch vagabonds be not speedily put to silence, as I trust they will be put to silence, by the good sense and the humanity and the justice of English gentlemen.

Tell Farmer Horne, or get Mr. Dean to tell him, that I say this is the sort of matter for him to lay before his congregation. Tell him that I say that it is a shame that the people of Normandy should be imposed upon by those who pretend to collect money for the "conversion of the heathen," which is false pretence, and a gross and infamous lie from the beginning to the end; tell him that I say that I am very *sorry* to see an honest and good man like him thus imposed upon. Tell him that not a farthing of the money is ever applied to the purposes of real religion and piety; and that the fellows who get the money into their hands up at London spend it upon themselves, or their wives, or their girls; and that not a farthing of it is ever applied to any good purpose.

Hoping that you and your family and all of you are well, and knowing that you will be glad to hear that I am the same.

I remain,
Your master and friend,
WM. COBBETT.

LETTER 9

Shangana Castle,
15 *Nov.* 1834

MARSHALL,

You must needs think that I hear about the FIRES that are going on in England. Indeed I see accounts of them in every newspaper that comes from England. There is no man more sorry than I am, that my country should be in such a state; but I cannot join with those who call the working people of England *"lazy and sturdy miscreants"*; being, besides, quite satisfied, that, to call them by such names, never yet was, and never will be, the way to make

them cease to do anything, in the doing of which they are
engaged, however wrong it may be to do that thing.

Now then, Marshall, so much for that; and now I have
to talk to you about another matter. You know that there
has been a POOR-LAW BILL passed, which, whenever it
shall be put into execution, will make *a total change* as to the
situation of the working people. It was a Scotchman of the
name of Brougham who proposed this bill to the House of
Lords; and he said that such a bill was necessary to
prevent the poor from SWALLOWING UP THE LORDS'
ESTATES. Now, Marshall, it is a command of God, that
those who have the ability to do it shall plead the cause of
the poor, the widow, the fatherless, and the stranger. I
have the ability to do this, as well as to teach you how to
rear fields of cabbages; and it is my duty to obey this
command, and not to waste my time in feasting and drinking, and in snoring in bed. After having taken time to
consider in what way I can best perform this duty, I have
determined to write and publish a LITTLE BOOK, in such
form and size that any working man can carry it in his
waistcoat pocket, and at the price of fifteen pence; so that
all the working men may read it, or hear it read. And I
shall have it bound in leather, so that it shall not easily be
worn out; and that it may be read, not only by the men of
the present day, but by their children, and their great-
great grandchildren. The Title and Contents of this little
book are as follows:

COBBETT'S

LEGACY TO LABOURERS;

or,

What is the Right which the Lords, Baronets, and 'Squires,
have to possess the Lands, or to make the Laws?

———

In Six Letters addressed to the Working People
of the whole Kingdom.

Letter I.   How came some men to have a greater
right to parcels of land than any other
men have to the same land?

95

Letter II. What right have English landlords to the lands? How came they in possession of them? Of what nature is their title?

Letter III. Is their right to the land *absolute?* Is the land their *own;* or, are they *holders* under a superior?

Letter IV. Have they *dominion* in their lands? Or do they lawfully possess only the *use* of them?

Letter V. Can they do *what they like* with their lands?

Can they *use* them in any way that shall clearly tend to the injury of other men, or to that of the King, or Commonwealth?

Can they *use* them so as to drive the natives from them?

Can they *use* them so as to cause the natives to perish of hunger, or of cold?

Letter VI. What right have the Lords, Baronets, 'Squires, and rich men, to *vote at elections* any more than working men have?

You are not to suppose, Marshall, that I am going to die, because I have awarded you a legacy. You are to have it first or last; and the sooner you have it the better; and if I see it in your hands in my life-time I shall be sure that you have got it. Since the vagabonds have dared to assert that the *poor have no rights*, it is high time to see what are the *rights of the rich.*

I have nothing more to say to you at present, only that, if all of you work as hard as I do; if you be as diligent (as I hope you are) with the ploughs and the spades and the dung-prongs and the billhooks as I am with the pen, you will have the farm in most excellent condition before I get back. I hope that all of you and your wives and families are well, and

I am,

Your master and friend,

WM. COBBETT.

Part 3

Cobbett's Proposals for Remedying the Wrongs

And for decades ministers, Members of Parliament and officials, often ill-informed, prejudiced and overworked, struggled in unfamiliar conditions to devise remedies for Ireland. Inevitably then, lack of foresight and initiative, blundering and much wasted effort, characterised government activity during the first half of the century. [R. B. McDowell.][1]

When he stood for election in 1831, Cobbett had put forward proposals for remedying the troubles in Ireland. What he saw in 1834 gave him no reason to modify those views: it strengthened his conviction that only truly radical measures, going far beyond anything proposed even by O'Connell and his associates could begin to make any impression on the lot of the Irish people.

In December 1831, three years before he went to Ireland, Cobbett gave a series of lectures in Manchester in which he explained to his audience fourteen propositions on which he wished to be elected to Parliament. They were nothing if not radical, among them being: the abolition of pensions and sinecures; the disbanding of the standing army and replacing it with local militias; the abolition of tithes and the selling of Crown property; the abolition of the National Debt with equitable adjustments to those who had lent money to the government; the substitution of taxes on landowners for the indirect taxes which fell so heavily on the poor. The fourteenth and last proposition dealt with Ireland and read as follows:

> To cause the PROTESTANT HIERARCHY to be legally repealed and abolished in Ireland; and to cause the Parliament of the whole kingdom to hold its sessions, and the King to hold his Court, in IRELAND once in every three years; and to cause the same to take place in the city of YORK once in every three years, and also in the city of SALISBURY once in every three years.

In introducing this proposition, Cobbett said:

> If all or any part of the former propositions were 'wild and visionary'; if these epithets were justly applicable to them, where will you be able to find epithets descriptive of the wildness of this proposition? I am, however, fortunately circumstanced here: I have to do with a patient that the doctors have given up; with that sort of patient of which the sons of the healing art say, 'Nothing more can be done for him: let him have just what he fancies'. In short, such is the state of Ireland, according even to the confessions of

the Government itself, that no suggestion relative to measures for making it better off than it is can be deemed presumptuous, be they what they may, and come from what source they may. Every one says that some great change in the affairs in Ireland is necessary; but no one attempts to say what change. Those who pour forth complaints in the name of Ireland, however just those complaints may be, and however able the organ of putting them forth, invariably confine themselves to making the complaints, to describing the injuries and the sufferings of Ireland, to suggesting evils to be remedied, but seldom or never do they suggest the remedy.

He then pointed out in further justification of his startling proposition, that for years he had been arguing that the granting of Emancipation would do nothing, in itself, to give Ireland either prosperity or tranquility.

As we approached the passing of the Emancipation Bill, I became more zealous in my endeavours to show that that bill would be of no use unless accompanied by poor-laws, and a repeal of the Protestant hierarchy. I was perfectly indefatigable in my endeavours to inculcate this belief. In opposition to my opinion was almost the whole of the press, as soon as the Duke of Wellington and Peel had been converted, by that miracle which so surprisingly operated upon their souls. While the bill was before the Houses of Parliament, I did my best to cause it to be passed; but never did I mention the subject without, at the same time, urging upon my readers the truth, that the bill would do nothing without abolishing the Protestant hierarchy and the introduction of the poor-laws. The very next year the discontents of Ireland were greater, and their consequences more dreadful than ever. Indeed it is perfectly notorious that the situation of Ireland has been growing worse and worse, and more and more replete with danger, ever since the passing of that famous bill

Now, as I so repeatedly and so fully and so distinctly repeated, all these consequences of that bill; as both the parties in Parliament most cordially joined in expressing their confident expectations of tranquillity and prosperity to Ireland being amongst the consequences of that measure; as Mr. O'Connell and Mr. Sheil, and the whole of the Catholic Association expressed the same expectations; and as upon the same ground they assented to the disfranchisement of the forty-shilling freeholders of Ireland, declaring that the bill was so great a good, was so high a prize, that it could not be purchased at too dear a rate: describing it as the bond of peace and union, as the rivetter of everlasting affection between England and Ireland; as this was the language of all these persons and parties, and as my language and my sentiments were precisely the opposite of these; and as the event has now proved that I was right, and that they were all wrong: these facts being notoriously true, I trust, gentlemen, that you will not deem it presumption that I now submit to you propositions which these same persons and parties will, in all probability, be as much disposed to censure as they were my opinions of 1828 and 1829.

Having thus prepared the ground, Cobbett went on to argue the case for his fourteenth proposition.

Gentlemen, *for what purpose* was this hierarchy established in Ireland? Must it not have been for the purpose of causing the people of Ireland to be Church Protestants? Upon what other ground could any men but ruthless tyrants have bestowed upon Protestant parsons and bishops those enormous revenues, which have of late years enabled some of the bishops to leave, at their death, each of them, upwards of £200,000 sterling? Yet at the end of about 250 years, this work of conversion has proceeded so slowly, that this church has not now to number in its flocks a seventh part of the inhabitants of the people at most; and, what is more, according to accounts which I have seen, and which I believe to be correct, its flocks are less numerous now than they were one hundred years ago. (In such circumstances) to uphold it is an act which posterity will certainly ascribe to nothing short of madness.

But without *poor-laws*, even this abolition of the hierarchy in Ireland would not produce tranquillity in the country; and what is more, it ought not to produce it, unless there be persons to contend that such an application ought to be made of the produce of a country, as to cause those who raise the produce, who create the produce, to experience periodical returns of hunger and

101

starvation. There has been great talk of the evils of absenteeism, as it is called, and certainly very great are these evils; but it is perfect nonsense to talk of putting an end to them, until the owners and occupiers of the land and the houses be compelled by law to leave a sufficiency of the produce for the destitute labourers. It is mortally injurious to Ireland that a large part of her produce should be sent out of the country, and its amount paid to absentees who expend that amount out of Ireland. This is a monstrous evil; it is the great source of the misery of the Irish people; and there is no remedy for it, but that of introducing and establishing the English poor law, which would withold from the absentees that part which they now take away to the injury of the country.

The last part of Cobbett's proposition concerned the removal of the Court and Parliament to Ireland once every three years. Cobbett hated London with its swarms of idlers and its ostentatious parading of luxury, and he wished 'to put a stop to the swellings of this enormous WEN'.

When it is considered that there is more human food actually wasted in and about the WEN, actually sent down the common sewers, flung into the dust-holes, than would support all the people in one of the considerable counties; when you consider these things, and look at the people of the WEN, as useless consumers of food and of clothing, brought together by the unnatural means of taxation, you must agree with me, that a dispersion of this monstrous mass must take place, before the nation can again know anything worthy of the name of prosperity.
    The meeting of the Parliament in Ireland would occasion twenty thousand English noblemen and gentlemen to go to Ireland, some one or other of whom would have his foot upon every square yard of the country in the course of six months. Let any one imagine the inevitable effects of this species of communication. Endless acts of benevolence would and must arise from the holding of the Court and the sitting of Parliament in Ireland. Ireland, with all its resources, would become well known to numerous persons of wealth going from England; and this is the way to introduce capital and improvement into Ireland.

The presence of the Court and the Parliament would overawe petty tyranny. The King's Ministers would be there to see the conditions and hear the grievances of his people; and the King and Parliament would be there upon the spot to redress those grievances: then the two countries would become one in deed as well as in name.

Such were Cobbett's views in 1831, and such his optimism. For the enormity of the misery he saw in Ireland three years later he was not prepared. Yet the very enormity spurred him to greater efforts, and within a month of his return he had completed the book he had promised Marshall in his letter to him of 15 November 1834.

This book, *Legacy to Labourers*, is perhaps the most serious of all his works. Cobbett's immediate reaction to the appalling conditions of the Irish poor was to fight, with all the strength remaining to him, to prevent such conditions occurring throughout the whole of the United Kingdom. His Letters from Ireland were, as we have seen, shot through with warnings that the conditions in Ireland could spread to rest of the kingdom unless strenuous efforts were made to prevent them. So Cobbett exerted all his powers to arm the working people to defend their rights. The arms he gave them were the answers to the six questions which he had set out at the end of his ninth letter to Marshall.[2]

Seen in the context of the time, *Legacy to Labourers* shouts defiance at prevailing opinions. The social philosophers whose influence was the greatest and whose theories lay behind the New Poor Laws were the laissezfaire economists of the schools of Adam Smith, Malthus and Ricardo, and the Utilitarian school led by Jeremy Bentham and James Mill. Although they differed in their initial premises, they can all be said to have believed in some degree that there was what Adam Smith termed 'a hidden hand' which regulated society. Strive as it might, government could do little to alter the powerful forces at work. One example of this 'hidden hand' is Malthus' theory that any bettering of the condition of the poor would inevitably result in an increase of population. This extra or 'surplus' population would result in a rise of prices because of increased demand, coupled with a lowering of wages because of the increased competition for employment. Poverty would return and government intervention was therefore useless. Small wonder that economics in the early nineteenth century was labelled the dismal science. The Utilitarians, whose avowed aim was 'the greatest happiness of the greatest number,' might at first glance seem to promise a more compassionate view of society. But the Utilitarian philosophers, although concerned for the well-being of all, believed, with the economists, that any interference with the hidden hand of the iron laws of supply and demand could only lead to a worsening of existing conditions; furthermore, they were reluctant to allow the labouring classes a say in government on the grounds that only the more educated section of the people were sufficiently 'enlightened' to determine what measures would be most likely to ensure the greatest happiness of the greatest number.

In contradiction to these widely held opinions, Cobbett believed that there was no hidden hand which drove each individual to seek his own pleasure and self-interest, but that man had within his own nature a propensity to care for others. Moreover, again unlike his contemporaries, he maintained that this propensity was as strong and probably even stronger in the labouring classes than in the so-called enlightened classes of society. After the gloomy pessimism and convoluted theories of Malthus and Ricardo, his writing breathes a very different spirit:

> Natural justice, without any law either of God or man, would dictate to those who possess the necessaries of life, to give (if they have more than absolutely necessary to support their own wants) some portion of them to prevent others from perishing. Even the animals, not human beings, take care of their young. A hen, which is become almost a skeleton from sitting, will come out in the

104

morning with her chickens, hungry as it is possible for her
to be; but not one morsel will she swallow till the chickens
be satisfied. She will break the victuals for them and,
though half famishing herself, will swallow none till they
have got enough. And who has ever seen a labouring man,
or his wife, not ready to endure, and frequently enduring,
the torments of hunger, rather than suffer their children to
want?

Before his visit to Ireland, Cobbett had attacked corruption,
peculation, hypocrisy, incompetence, greed and cruelty. He
had never been afraid of naming those whom he thought
responsible for the evils of society, but he had been careful to
refrain from inciting rebellion. Cobbett was not a revolutionary. Though he sympathised with those who rebelled against
intolerable conditions, he consistently urged the use of con-
stitutional methods to redress wrongs. But Parliamentary
Reform, for which he had striven for so long, had resulted in
little change. Apart from a handful of Radicals and an
increase in the number of O'Connell's followers, the same
faces were to be seen in the Commons after the Reform Act
as before. The provisions of the Act of 1832 had included
neither universal suffrage nor the ballot, and bribery and
intimidation were as rampant at election time after the
Reform Act as ever they were before it. It was the 'Reformed'
Parliament which had passed the New Poor Laws, and it
was the 'Reformed' Parliament that was even now passing
yet more stringent coercion acts to subdue the Irish people
and to enforce the collection of tithes from a starving people.

What Cobbett had seen in Ireland persuaded him that he
must now openly call into question the assumptions which
lay behind the ownership of land and property. In his Introduction to *Legacy to Labourers*, he stated that until then he
had forborne to touch upon the question of private property.
But now, he wrote:

it would be the extreme of baseness on my part, to forbear
any longer. MALTHUS'S crew, with BROUGHAM at
their head, are calling incessantly for 'COARSER FOOD'

for the labourer; for separating him from his wife, and both from children, and for putting dresses of disgrace on all of them, if they happen to be poor and destitute; they are doing this upon the express ground that it is necessary to preserve the estates of landlords; and therefore it is, that I inquire, *what is the right which these landlords have to those estates?*

The gist of Cobbett's argument in his *Legacy to Labourers* is that access to a portion of the wealth of the land he dwells in is the birthright of every member of society. If government can call on its members to obey its laws, to defend the realm, and to pay taxes to maintain the state, that government has an obligation to ensure to all its citizens an adequate portion of the wealth the country produces. Throughout the six chapters which make up the book, Cobbett quotes passage after passage from the Old and the New Testaments to support his belief that the labourer is worthy of his hire, that he must never be sent away empty-handed, and that widows, orphans and the destitute have an inalienable right to relief from the state. The law of God, the whole spirit of the British Constitution as interpreted by lawyers throughout the ages, and natural justice, Cobbett maintained, are unanimous in declaring it to be the duty of government to protect and succour those who suffer from oppression. Yet even the Protestant churches, established and dissenters alike, seemed to acquiesce in the enormities that were being perpetrated on the poor and preaching to them that they should accept and be contented with their lot.

The appalling results of flouting the laws of God, of the spirit of the Constitution, and of natural justice, Cobbett described as follows:

It has, of late years, been a wide-spread practice in Ireland and Scotland, to drive the working people off the lands for the purpose of laying the lands down into pasturage for cattle or for sheep; by which means the landlord calculates that he gets more in clear profit by driving the people off than by letting them remain.

He then went on to quote from a report on the results of one of these land clearings in Ireland which a Committee of the House of Commons had submitted to Parliament in July 1830. This report had stated that 'it would be impossible for language to convey' the state of distress, disease and misery into which the tenants had been plunged after eviction. Deprived of land and livelihood, they migrated to towns where they were obliged to theft and 'all manner of vice and iniquity' in order to procure subsistence. The report ended by stating the 'painful' fact that 'a vast number of them had perished from want'.

Spurning the non-interventionist theories of the 'feelosophers', Cobbett thundered:

> This (report) appears to have excited no wonder at all; there was no one talked of any measure to prevent a repetition of this. Quite a proper thing, to all appearances. No servant of the king to assert his rights of dominion, and of his claim to the safety of the lives of his subjects; nothing said to this clearing proprietor any more than if he had been a god.
>
> If the landlords have a right, be the pretence what it may, to eject the natives from the land; if they have a right, taking the whole body of them together, to turn one single family out upon the bare ground, *without providing for them another place of abode*, then they have the RIGHT OF KILLING; and this, too, in the face of the law, which declares that constant protection from birth to death, is due from the state to every man, as the sole foundation of its claim to allegiance.

A realist, uninfluenced by the communal theories of the early socialists such as those of his contemporaries Robert Owen and the Irishman William Thompson, Cobbett accepted the institution of private ownership of land. He did, however, question the mystique surrounding the landed aristocracy. Should those who traced their titles and estates back to the Norman Conquest be proud of an ancestor who had invaded, despoiled and robbed the native population of

107

Britain of their inheritance? For those who had been given their titles and estates during Reformation times, his 'History of the Protestant Reformation' was condemnation enough. As for the new lords, created in such numbers by Pitt, were they not often men who had bought their titles and estates with money gained from speculating in the public funds, or, in other words, by gambling and usury?[3] The prescriptive right of landlords to do what they wished with their lands was, for Cobbett, as questionable as the prescriptive right of the Church to its tithes and estates which he had queried earlier. Some inequalities in wealth, ownership and ability, Cobbett believed to be inevitable. What he would not accept were the gross inequalities manifested in the growth of ever larger estates and the absence of laws to compel landowners to shoulder their responsibilities to those who were not only less fortunate than themselves, but upon whose labour the whole of society depended.

While Cobbett was writing his *Legacy to Labourers*, the Whig ministry which had been in power since 1830 had been replaced by a Tory government under Sir Robert Peel. Although in the early nineteenth century party divisions were not so clearly drawn as today, Cobbett had even less sympathy with the Tories than with the Whigs. Peel had been strongly opposed to Catholic Emancipation all his life until he had been converted by that 'miracle' Cobbett spoke of in his Manchester Lecture on Ireland. His conversion had occurred only because he believed Emancipation would avert civil war, but as Cobbett had foreseen civil war was now nearer than ever before. Extremely ugly incidents involving large numbers of tithe protesters had broken out all over Ireland and repressive acts were now more necessary than before Emancipation. Nor were Peel's mistaken policies regarding Ireland Cobbett's only quarrel with him, for the new Prime Minister had opposed Parliamentary Reform and was one of the staunchest supporters of the New Poor Laws.

So, having completed *Legacy to Labourers*, Cobbett began

in January 1835 to print in his Political Register a series of Open Letters to the new Prime Minister which he subsequently collected together and published under the title *Legacy to Peel*. They dealt with a variety of topics and the second was entitled: What Will You Do With Ireland, and Particularly With The Church of Ireland? Outraged by what he had seen during his tour, Cobbett spelt out in unequivocal terms the origins of that Church of Ireland which he wished to see disestablished. Referring to the attempts by England to force the native Irish to abjure their old religion and embrace Protestantism during the reign of 'that tigress', Elizabeth, Cobbett wrote:

> That country became a scene such as the world never before beheld. The hardiest parsons that could be found; the most daring, and most merciless, were sent over to take possession of the livings. When they opened their Prayer Book the people screamed, and ran from them. She attacked the country by piecemeal: the people were dragged into the churches by force, sometimes tied hand and foot, and laid down upon the floor, while the reading and the preaching were going on. She had constant war in Ireland: constant pretended rebellion; constant confiscation and bloodshed; but never thought of poor-laws for Ireland! Indeed that country was given up as spoil to her rapacious courtiers. When cruelties unheard of, and bloodshed to redden the ground had subdued the people into something like quiet for awhile, agents were sent amongst them for the express purpose of stirring up resistance. This was termed rebellion. Attainders and forfeitures ensued; and away went half a county at a time from the possessors by descent of seven or eight hundred years, into the hands of the greatest miscreants that had ever dishonoured the face of the earth.

     *   *   *   *   *

Is it any wonder, then, that every native Irishman should have a sort of antipathy against England herself? I do not like to hear Mr. O'Connell lay the blame upon 'England', because, in the first place, I am an Englishman myself; and I always feel some portion of the dishonour which is justly imputed to my country. I am not guilty, in this case, and all Ireland well knows it; but still the accusation is unpleasant to my ears. Yet, though I hear these accusations of Mr. O'Connell with regret, I cannot say that they are unjust; and, certainly, it would be unnatural in an Irishman not to entertain the resentful feeling, however strongly prudence might plead with him not to express it. I used to blame Mr. O'Connell more on account of these expressions, till I saw Ireland with my own eyes. So far from blaming him now, I honour him for these marks of his deep-felt resentment; and I deem that Irishman either an ignorant man, or a base villain, who does not applaud him for every effort that he is making in behalf of his country, so long and so cruelly oppressed.

Cobbett ended this letter with a direct appeal to the Prime Minister.

If you cannot do anything material directly, you might avoid everything calculated to augment the evil. The Catholic Emancipation Bill placed Catholics and Protestants upon a level with regard to fitness for emolument and power; but this only adds to the irritation arising from exclusion, if the provisions of the law be rendered of *non-effect*. The Orange power is nearly as dominant as it ever was. This is the great and just ground of complaint. One of my first acts should be battering down the statue of WILLIAM THE THIRD, which is painted up by the Orangemen in insolent triumph of impunity to injustice. My next act should be to compel the residence of landholders, or forfeiture of rents to a certain extent, according to the nature of the case. I would take care, I warrant you, that the people of Ireland should not toil to furnish money to enrich the wretches of PARIS, of MILAN, and of ROME. I would take care that effectual provision should be made for the relief of the destitute, and not suffer Ireland to be peopled with farmers who never taste meat from year's end to year's end, while twenty thousand oxen, sheep and hogs are shipped from her shores every week in the year.

It is said that capital is wanted in Ireland. The capital is in the land; the land produces twenty times as much as the people consume; I mean those who work upon the land;

but how is there to be capital in Ireland, if all the fruits are taken away? This talk about 'capital' is like all the rest of the botheration stuff which we hear from the at once sly and brazen Irish landlords who, after making the working people pay for the sea-weed that is drifted upon the shore, and who bring the money over, swallowing the price of a car-load in one gulp of turtle soup, tell us, with a sort of wise simper, 'What we want in Ireland, Mr. Cobbett, is CAPITAL'.

It is for you, sir, to make Ireland abound with a sufficiency of capital. It has been formed by nature to be as happy as any country beheld by the sun in his whole course. It has the mildest of climates, the richest of soils, mountains green to their tips. It is by nature agricultural, though the greedy beasts that rob it are crying out for manufactories. In short, God seems to have done every thing to make its inhabitants happy, and man seems to have done every thing to make them miserable; and it is your bounden duty, and the duty of every man who at all meddles with public affairs, to neglect nothing within his power, now to undo all the mischiefs which England has inflicted upon this valuable part of his Majesty's dominions.

This letter was published on 26 January 1835, and the series of letters to Peel continued until the end of February. Cobbett's output in these last months of his life was prodigious. He followed the first two Legacies with a third, the *Legacy to Parsons*. Aware that his arguments for abolishing the 'prescriptive' rights of the Church of Ireland to its revenues could be applied equally to the Church of England, Cobbett boldly pressed the argument to its logical conclusion. He addressed this Legacy to the Bishop of London because he had been amongst the foremost of the peers in the Lords to press for the New Poor Laws with their coarser food clauses and harsh conditions in the workhouses to deter the poor from applying for relief. Cobbett stated his purpose in these words:

It is now become a question, seriously, publicly, and practically entertained, whether you and your brethren of the

111

Established Church should be legally deprived of all your enormous temporal possessions; and also, whether your whole order should not, as a thing supported by the law, be put an end to for ever.

Cobbett's Irish experience led him to answer that question in the affirmative.

The three Legacies, to Labourers, to Peel and to Parsons, amounting to over one hundred thousand words, were produced between December 1834 and March 1835. Such an output, combined with the work of running his farm in the country and attending Parliament was too much even for a man of Cobbett's spirit and physique. His last appearance in the House of Commons was on 25 May, when he spoke and voted on a motion on Agricultural Distress. After that late session he went down to his farm in Surrey seriously ill and within a few weeks he was dead. The description of his last hours published in a black-bordered edition of his great paper *The Political Register*, and written by one of his sons has often been quoted:

On Wednesday, he could no longer remain shut up from the fields, but desired to be carried round the farm; which being done, he criticized the work that had been going on in his absence, and detected some little deviation from his orders, with all the quickness that was so remarkable in him. As he was carried to see the fields, a little boy in a blue smock-frock happened to come by us, to whom my father gave a laughing look, at which I thought I should have dropped, I knowing what was passing in his mind. He seemed refreshed at the sight of the little creature, which he had once so precisely resembled, though now at such an immeasurable distance. On Wednesday night he grew more and more feeble, and was evidently sinking; but he continued to answer with perfect clearness every question that was put to him. In the last half-hour, his eyes became dim; and at ten minutes after one p.m., he leaned back, closed them as if to sleep, and died without a gasp.

Not one of Cobbett's recommendations for Ireland was acted

upon. The Church of Ireland continued to draw its great revenues; the Orange Ascendancy continued to hold most of the positions of power; the statue of William III continued to stand in Parliament Square in Dublin 'in insolent triumph of impunity to injustice'; and right up to and indeed throughout the terrible famine years of 1845–48, food poured out of Ireland to enrich the 'wretches of Paris, of Milan and of Rome'. When poor-laws were introduced into Ireland three years after Cobbett's death, they were based on all the harsh conditions against which he had cried out in Parliament and in the press.

In this sense it would be true to say that Cobbett's intervention into the Irish scene was a failure. Even the influence he undoubtedly exercised during the fight for Catholic Emancipation turned against his concern for Ireland. Only his arguments for restoring to Catholics the right to vote and stand for Parliament were used. His warnings that emancipation without the disestablishment of the Church of Ireland and the introduction of poor-laws were ignored and the consequences of the bill were disastrous.

In another sense, too, he failed. The anathema pronounced on him by O'Connell, 'Let not the name of this beast, (for man I will not call him) be ever again mentioned . . .' seems still to hang over Cobbett's writings on Ireland. Although both Cobbett and O'Connell made ample and generous recompense for their earlier denunciations of one another, and although O'Connell travelled down from Westminster to follow Cobbett's body to his grave in Farnham churchyard, posterity has been less kind. Most of his biographers and most of his admirers pass over his championship of the Irish people. Only once, since their appearance in *The Political Register*, have Cobbett's *Letters from Ireland* been reprinted. G. D. H. Cole included them in his edition of *Rural Rides*, but that edition has long been out of print. Perhaps for English readers, his outspoken condemnation of centuries of English misrule is too harsh and too uncompromising to be

113

palatable. Better, surely, to concentrate on his love for England, to think of him as a man who praised her laws and her constitution; better to forget that underlying all his lyrical descriptions of England in *Rural Rides* is his detestation of the hideous perversions to which those laws and that constitution were contorted during his lifetime.

Cobbett is admired as a man who loved his country. It would, I believe, be more true of him to say that he was a man who loved country people. Wherever he went, in Canada or in France, in the United States or in Scotland, in Ireland or in England, he found the same virtues amongst those who worked the land. Born of country stock, living and working exclusively amongst them until he came of age, and always returning to physical work on his farm whenever his duties allowed him, Cobbett's identification with the working classes never left him. Sufficient food, sufficient raiment and sufficient shelter for those who laboured, with generous provision for the aged, the widowed, the infirm and those unable to find employment, was his recipe for discontent. It was because he believed that 'want, horrid want was the great parent of crime', that he defended the Irish people against all the allegations of savagery and lawlessness directed against them and cried out against the bullets and bayonets that were sent to stifle their discontent.

He wished to be remembered, not as he is remembered, as a writer who conjures up for later generations an England that is no more, but as a man who championed the cause of and believed in the goodness of working people. When, white hot from his searing experience in Ireland, he produced his *Legacy to Labourers*, priced it at fifteen pence, and bound it as he had promised Marshall, so that it would fit into a workman's pocket, he wrote in the introduction how he wished to be remembered. Seeming to sense that his end was near, he explained why he had called it a Legacy. It was, he said, because he hoped that after he had been laid under the turf, the little book:

114

will remind the working people, whenever they shall read it, or see it, or hear of it, that they once had a friend whom neither the love of gain on the one hand, nor the fear of loss on the other, could seduce from his duty towards God, towards his country, and towards them; will remind them that that friend was born in a cottage and bred to the plough; men mighty in power were thirty-four years endeavouring to destroy him; that in spite of this he became a Member of Parliament, freely chosen by the sensible and virtuous and spirited people of Oldham; and that his name was

WILLIAM COBBETT.

Notes

Notes to the Introduction

1. Daniel O'Connell, original letter reproduced in: Maire and Conor Cruise O'Brien, *A Concise History of Ireland*, London 1972, 101.
2. William Hazlitt, *The Character of Cobbett*, London 1821: 'He is a kind of *fourth estate* in the country. He is not only unquestionably the most powerful political writer of the present day, but one of the best writers in the country.'
3. William Cobbett, *A Grammar of the English Language*, London 1818.

Notes to Part 1

1. Walter Scott, quoted in: C. Maxwell, *Strangers in Ireland*, London 1954.
2. William Cobbett, *The Life and Adventures of Peter Porcupine*, Philadelphia 1796.
3. *Porcupine's Works*, I: *A Summary View of the Politics of the United States*, 1801.
4. *Porcupine's Works*, I: *A Bone to Gnaw for the Democrats*, 1795.
5. *Porcupine's Works*, X: *Porcupine's Gazette*, June 1799.
6. *Porcupine's Works*, X: *Porcupine's Gazette*, June 1799.
7. *Political Register*, IV, 13–20 August 1803.
8. *Political Register*, IV, 10–17 December 1803.
9. *Political Register*, VII, 2 March 1805.
10. G. K. Chesterton, *Cobbett*, London 1928.
11. *Political Register*, LXXXIV, March 1834.
12. *Political Register*, XVI, 9 December 1809.
13. *Political Register*, XVI, 9 December 1809.
14. *Political Register*, XVII, 12 May 1810.
15. *Political Register*, XVII, 12 May 1810.
16. *Political Register*, XXIX, 21 October 1815.
17. Thomas Carlyle, in: P. Newberry (ed.), *Rescued Essays of Thomas Carlyle*, London.
18. *Political Register*, IX, 15 March 1806.
19. William Carleton, *The Black Prophet*, London 1899[2].
20. The population of Ireland was divided into three disparate religious groups. One tenth, the Protestant Ascendancy, were members of the Established Church: they alone could hold positions under the Crown, enter the professions, and stand for Parliament. Over two thirds were Catholics, native Irish who had been dispossessed of their lands during

the sixteenth and seventeenth centuries. The remainder, about one fifth, were Dissenters: most of these lived in the northern province of Ulster. Although the Dissenters played a leading part in the rebellion of 1798, after the rebellion they began to be loyalists, that is, they wished to retain the link with Britain because Britain would uphold their claim to be the rightful proprietors of their lands. The possibility that this right might be called into question if ever the Union between Britain and Ireland were repealed exacerbated the hostility between Dissenters and Catholics in the north.

21. Elie Halévy, *A History of the English People in 1815*, trans. E. I. Watkin and D. A. Baker, London 1924.
22. Edward Wakefield, *An Account of Ireland: Statistical and Political*, London 1812.
23. Elie Halévy, op. cit.
24. *Political Register*, IX, 9 March 1806.
25. *Political Register*, XII, 29 August 1807.
26. *Political Register*, LXXII, 18 June 1831.
27. *Political Register*, XLII, 1 June 1822.
28. *Political Register*, XVIII, 10 November 1810.
29. *Political Register*, XXX, 4 May 1816.
30. *Political Register*, XXX, 4 May 1816.
31. R. B. McDowell, *Public Opinion and Government Policy in Ireland, 1801–1848*, London 1952.
32. The victory of William III, who, as William of Orange, had been called to the throne to succeed James II, gave rise to the terms 'Orange' and 'Orangemen'. To celebrate the victory of the Protestant King over the exiled Catholic James, a statue of William III was erected in Parliament Square, Dublin, and it was decorated with orange ribbons on each anniversary of the Battle of the Boyne. The word 'Orange', meaning Protestant, is still used to this day.
33. *Porcupine's Works*, IV: *Life and Adventures of Peter Porcupine*, 1789.
34. William Cobbett, *A History of the Protestant Reformation*, London 1824.
35. G. K. Chesterton, *Cobbett*, London 1928.
36. William Cobbett, *A History of the Protestant Reformation*, London 1824.
37. G. D. H. Cole, *The Life of William Cobbett*, Glasgow and London 1924.
38. William Cobbett, *A History of the Protestant Reformation*, London 1824.
39. ibid.

40. See 'On Rebellion and Repression' above.
41. In 1810 Cobbett had been fined and imprisoned for two years in Newgate, for seditious writing. In 1817, fearing a second prosecution, he fled to America, where he continued to write his *Political Register* from Long Island. Details of his life and the events surrounding it are given in the Biographical Summary below.
42. *Political Register*, XXIII, 6 February 1813.
43. *Political Register*, XXIII, 6 February 1813.
44. *Political Register*, XVII, 20 January 1810.
45. J. C. Beckett, *The Making of Modern Ireland*, London 1966.
46. Richard Pares, *George III and the Politicians*, Oxford 1953.
47. *Political Register*, XXIII, 15 May 1813.
48. Gearoid O'Tuathaig, *Ireland before the Famine*, Dublin 1972.
49. Lewis Melville, *The Life and Letters of William Cobbett*, London 1913.
50. *Political Register*, LV, 13 August 1825.
51. *Political Register*, LIII, 19 March 1825.
52. *Political Register*, LIV, 21 May 1825.
53. *Political Register*, LIV, 21 May 1825.
54. *Political Register*, LV, 23 July 1825.
55. *Political Register*, LV, 13 August 1825.
56. *Political Register*, LV, 24 September 1825.
57. *Political Register*, LXVI, 20 December 1828.
58. *Political Register*, LVI, 12 July 1828.
59. *Political Register*, LVI, 26 July 1828.
60. *Political Register*, LXVII, 21 February 1829.
61. *Political Register*, LXVII, 21 February 1829.
62. *Political Register*, LXVII, 7 February 1829.
63. *Political Register*, LXVIII, 29 August 1829.
64. J. Mitchel, *The History of Ireland*, Dublin 1869.
65. *Political Register*, LXXV, 18 February 1832.
66. *Political Register*, LXXV, 18 February 1832.
67. *Cobbett's Manchester Lectures*, 1832.
68. *Political Register*, LXXIX, 16 February 1833.
69. *Political Register*, LXXIX, 16 February 1833.
70. *Political Register*, LXXIX, 16 February 1833.
71. *Political Register*, LXXIX, 16 March 1833.
72. *Political Register*, LXXXV, 27 September 1834.
73. *Cobbett's Manchester Lectures*, 1832.
74. G. D. H. Cole, *The Life of William Cobbett*, Glasgow and London 1924.
75. *Political Register*, LXXV, 21 January 1832.
76. *Political Register*, LXXXV, 26 July 1834.

Notes to Part 2

1. Most of Cobbett's Letters from Ireland are reproduced here in full. Where they contain matter pertaining only to England, those passages have been omitted.

Notes to Part 3

1. R. B. McDowell, *Public Opinion and Government Policy in Ireland: 1801–46*, London 1952.
2. See end of Part 2 above.
3. It is interesting to note here that Cobbett is one of the few men who boasted that his grandfather was a day-labourer, not in order to prove that he had risen from humble beginnings, but to dissociate himself from the taint of being descended from a robber, a court toady, or a usurer.

BIOGRAPHICAL SUMMARY

Date	Age	Some Events in Cobbett's Life	Date	Major Events mentioned in Text
1763		William Cobbett born, third of four sons of a small farmer, in Farnham, Surrey. He worked on his father's farm until	1690	Exiled James II defeated by William III at Battle of the Boyne.
			1702	First of series of Penal Laws against the Catholics depriving them of all political rights.
1783	20	he left home and, wishing to see the world, enlisted as a private soldier.	1775	Daniel O'Connell born.
1785	22	Cobbett served with his regiment in Canada and rose to the rank of Sergeant-Major.	1775 –83	American War of Independence.
1791	28	When regiment returned home, Cobbett obtained honourable discharge. Married.	1789	Outbreak of French Revolution.
1792	29	Cobbett went to France to study the language. Foreseeing French–English war, left after 6 months and settled in Philadelphia; earned living by teaching English to Frenchmen fleeing Revolution.	1791	Wolf Tone, a Protestant barrister, founded the United Irishman which aimed at radical reform.
			1793	Execution of Louis XVI. Bloody stage of French Revolution. France declared war on Britain (anti-Jacobin war) Catholic Relief Act for Ireland abolishing most of the Penal Laws and giving Catholics the vote, but still forbidding them to stand for Parliament or obtain high office.

Year	Age	Cobbett's life
1794	31	Cobbett published his first pamphlet in U.S. denouncing the French Revolution and supporting England in her war with the French Republic. From this time, he earned his living as a writer, under the name of Peter Porcupine.
1795	32	First of Cobbett's seven children born.
1800	37	Cobbett returned to England.
1802	39	Cobbett founded The Political Register.
1803	40	Cobbett published the Juverna letters in his Register, which led to his trial and a fine of £500 in the following year.
1810	47	Cobbett fined £1000 and imprisoned for two years for seditious writing. He continued to publish The Political Register from prison.
1814	51	Last of Cobbett's seven children born.
1817	54	Fearing a second prosecution, Cobbett fled to the U.S. where he continued to publish The Political Register from Long Island.
1819	56	Cobbett returned to England.

Year	Historical events
1796 and 1797	Attempts by French Republic to send troops to Ireland to aid the United Irishmen. Both times bad weather prevented their landing.
1798	Rising of the United Irishmen. 'The Great Rebellion'. French troops landed in Killda Bay to aid the rebellion.
1800	Act of Union between Britain and Ireland. Dissolution of Irish Parliament, and its absorption into Westminster Parliament.
1803	Napolean made First Consul of France. (Anti-Jacobin became Napoleonic War). Emmet's rebellion in Dublin.
1810	George III declared insane. George, Prince of Wales, became Prince Regent.
1813	Bill for Catholic Emancipation proposed by Gratton. Defeated.
1815	End of British–French war by defeat of Napoleon at Waterloo.
1817	Widespread failure of potato-crop in Ireland. Famine.

Date	Age	Some Events in Cobbett's Life	Date	Major Events mentioned in Text
1820	57	Cobbett stood for election at Coventry. Defeated.	1820	Death of George III. Prince Regent succeeded as George IV.
1821	58	Cobbett began his tour of England and published his findings in *The Political Register* for the next nine years.	1821	Bill for Catholic Emancipation proposed by Plunkett. Defeated in Lords, though passed in Commons.
			1823	O'Connell founded the Catholic Association in Ireland to press for Emancipation
1824	61	Cobbett published *The History of the Reformation*.		
1826	63	Cobbett stood for election at Preston. Defeated.		
			1828	O'Connell elected as Member of Parliament for Clare County, but unable to take his seat because he was a Catholic.
			1829	Catholic Emancipation Bill passed. O'Connell seated in Parliament. Forty shilling Irish freeholders disenfranchised.
1830	67	Cobbett published *Rural Rides* in book form.	1830	O'Connell founded Society for the Repeal of the Union.
1832	69	Cobbett elected as Member of Parliament. Toured north of England, and Scotland.	1832	Reform Bill passed extending the franchise and creating new seats in Parliament, particularly for the new industrial towns in the north of England. 'Tithe War' reached its height in Ireland.
1833	69	Cobbett took his seat in the Commons in January.		
1834	71	Cobbett toured Ireland.		
1835	72	Cobbett died.		
			1846 –8	The Great Famine in Ireland caused by nation-wide failure of potato-crop which led to the death by starvation and pestilence of approximately one million Irish poor.